LOOKING AT ADVENT

LOOKING
AT ADVENT

BRIAN HAYMES

First published 1989
Reprinted 1992
International Bible Reading Association
Robert Denholm House
Nutfield, Redhill, Surrey RH1 4HW

British Library Cataloguing in Publication Data
Haymes, Brian
  Looking at Advent
  1. Christian Church. Advent
  I. Title
  263'.91

ISBN 0-7197-0684-X

Typeset by Avonset, Midsomer Norton, Bath, Avon
Printed and bound by Cox & Wyman Ltd, Reading

To my Mother and Father-in-law

CONTENTS

Preface

I recall from my days of ministry in local congregations the frustration I felt as the season of Advent, with all its important themes, was overtaken by Christmas. I am grateful, therefore, to the International Bible Reading Association for the encouragement they have given me in the writing of this book. Its purpose is to help Christians reflect on some aspects of the faith that are easily neglected. I hope that by this means they will make that faith more fully their own.

I am grateful to the IBRA editorial staff for all their patient help and to Jenny Haymes and Rhoda Smith who did much of the typing.

Brian Haymes
June 1989

1
Advent time

'There is,' said the Preacher, 'a time for every matter under heaven' (Ecclesiastes 3.1b). All things have their rightful place in God's purposes and the Preacher went on to mention birth, death, planting, reaping, weeping, laughing and much else. Everything has its appropriate and proper time.

Time is a limited commodity for us all. That is what makes it so valuable. Sometimes we try to **buy** time. We are cross with ourselves when we **waste** time. Then we promise to be more self-disciplined and **save** time in the hope that we will have **more** time. But the fact is that each minute has only sixty seconds, each hour consists of sixty minutes and twenty-four remains the constant number of hours in any one day. The Preacher believed that there is enough time for everything that really matters in life. Perhaps what is important is that, like musicians playing in an orchestra, we **keep** time.

Someone once asked a famous conductor what you had to know to be able to play the loud cymbals. The answer was, 'When'! Doing the right thing at the wrong moment can be embarrassing – or worse. There is a time to embrace, but not while you are driving your car! There is a time for uproarious laughter, but not when someone has just heard tragic news. There is a time to day-dream, but not as you are sitting your examinations. A wise person **knows** the time.

Keeping in time is a useful phrase because so much of our everyday existence has its rhythms. In nature there is a time to plant and a time to reap. Each day has its rhythm of morning, noon and night. The Bible affirms that there is a proper rhythm for work and rest (Exodus 20.8–11). And the seasons, even in the British weather, keep to the four-beat time of spring, summer, autumn and winter.

Along with this natural order that shapes our lives we also keep in time with other dates and occasions that have personal or corporate significance. We celebrate birthdays, wedding anniversaries and other moments of importance. Nationally, November 5 is remembered by the English, January 25 by the Scots and all who love the writing of Robert Burns, while the Americans keep July 4 in recognition of their Declaration of Independence. Such anniversaries vary in their significance, of course, but they are part of our identity. Keeping a calendar is more than just ordering time and fixing dates.

By keeping a calendar, especially of those important personal and family occasions, we learn and remember who we are. We have roots in history and our personal self-understanding is enriched by informed remembering. This is an important matter, for example, for Jewish families. Each week they keep the celebration of Sabbath and every year they participate in the annual festivals in which the whole community, young and old, have parts to play. By this means their Jewish identity and faith are kept alive. The rising generation comes to know who they are. A failure in keeping these times could lead to a loss of identity.

Not everything in the past is worth remembering of course. Some things are better forgotten and perhaps Guy Fawkes Day (November 5) comes into that category. But for us all – individuals, families, nations – there are dates, times and seasons we cannot forget without losing a sense of who we are. Forgetting a birthday or wedding anniversary can be a slip of the memory and very embarrassing; but it may say something more about how relationships are perceived.

The Christian calendar

In the light of all this it is not surprising to learn that the Christian Church, from the earliest days, has kept a calendar. It has not always kept it in the same way and there have been plenty of local variations, but the Church has known the necessity of keeping in step with the gospel rhythms. Christmas, Easter, Pentecost – these have been special festival times. Can you imagine what would happen if these key events were forgotten? Almost certainly it would mean that Christians were losing something of their faith and their identity.

Many churches do not lay much emphasis on the festival of Pentecost – Whitsun. Is this one reason why we are so unclear and cautious when it comes to the doctrine of the Holy Spirit? Caring for the calendar is a form of faith health care. A community that celebrates Christmas and Easter without a similar emphasis on Pentecost may cease to live the trinitarian faith. What must it be like to travel in a three-wheeler car when one of the tyres is flat?

The Church has in fact not only developed a calendar of faith and worship that marks the crucial central festival days, but it has also worked out a whole Christian Year in which the content of the faith is remembered and celebrated in worship. This finds particular expression in lectionaries – series of Bible readings, carefully chosen, so that through the Christian

Year the whole story of the faith is proclaimed. By following the calendar and lectionary the Church is confronted regularly by the major doctrines of the faith. This is a proper discipline for preachers, and means that none of the great themes are avoided just because they are difficult, demanding or simply unfashionable.

There is a real wisdom in the Church faithfully keeping the Christian Year. Traditionally this has begun with Advent. Then comes the festival of Christmas followed by Epiphany, Jesus' baptism, Lent, Passion Sunday, Palm Sunday, Holy Week, Good Friday, the festival of Easter, Ascension Day, the festival of Pentecost, Trinity Sunday and the life of the Church. Within this broad plan there has emerged many local variations, but a congregation keeping this calendar would hear a full proclamation of the faith.

The importance of Advent

This book is particularly concerned with the season of Advent, its meaning, and the proclamation of its message. The Advent season covers four weeks in the contemporary calendar of Western churches – the four weeks before Christmas. The themes of these four weeks are important in themselves, bearing witness to significant aspects of the Christian faith. However, increasingly, Christmas has crept into Advent in two ways:

● First, Christians rightly share the excitement of Christmas. The festival services of worship are obviously very important and we want them to be the best that they can be. This takes preparation and preparation takes time. So choirs, drama groups, readers and many others find they have their minds on

Christmas well before we get there. Rehearsals begin very early, quite rightly so, but a price is being paid. It is that of overlooking the Advent message. That message is, of course, the true context of Christmas. There are features of the faith we are in danger of overlooking in our haste to celebrate Christmas.

● The second way, in which Advent is overtaken for many of us, is straightforwardly commercial. Father Christmas arrives as early as October in many of the big stores. From then on the great advertising machine accelerates, pushing Christmassy images into our consciousness through papers, magazines and television commercials. We spend and spend in our expectations of having a good time. And so it is that Christmas seems to start earlier and earlier each year.

A mother wrote in a church newspaper about the difficulties of keeping her children's attention, her own and that of her husband's fixed on the **Christian** significance of Christmas. Her article was a plea for the proper recognition of Advent in the Church, a plea which this book hears and to which it is trying to respond.

There may be another reason why Advent is not so well observed among us. It is that the themes of Advent are difficult for the preacher and for the congregation. Strange images of judgement and hope, which often seem very remote from our contemporary world, are set before us in the Bible and have to be wrestled with. The challenge of judgement, written deep into the Old and New Testaments, jars against our dangerously easy and sometimes sentimental proclamation of the love of God. Some of the Bible readings for Advent are theologically hard and pastorally unattractive; and so, understandably enough, we are tempted to hurry on to the baby in the manger.

All of this has serious consequences for the faith we hold and the life we live. Advent themes affirm essential aspects of the faith. Theologians speak of these doctrines under the title of **eschatology** – which means they are concerned with the 'last things', with God's final purposes, judgement, hell, heaven, death and the coming of Christ, past, present and future. The moral and ethical implications of these doctrines alone are enormous as we shall discover in later chapters. It is when the Christian Church has been particularly hard pressed and painfully aware of the costliness of sharing God's mission that the Advent message has been heard most urgently, powerfully and with deep thankfulness. All this is part of the good news of God; and to overlook these themes, by failing to give them due attention, is unnecessarily to impoverish ourselves.

Watching and waiting

Let us see if an exercise in imagination can begin to take us into the feel of these affirmations. Picture a young man standing in the foyer of a theatre. He is carefully dressed and just a little tense in his manner. He keeps looking at his watch every two or three minutes. Surely his memory is not that bad. He walks to the theatre door, looks out, and then back in again. As the time goes on, so his activity increases. He is waiting to meet a young lady. This is their first date. It took him a great deal of courage to ask her out. When will she come?

As we observe him we realise that all his life in these moments – all the glancing at the watch, the peering down the street, the constant shuffling of the feet – is dominated and determined by the hope of her coming. The expected and promised future meeting is even now actively giving form to his life. His hopes of happiness are focused on her coming. That may be a future event but it has powerful effect on the young man **now**.

So much of the Bible – Old and New Testaments – breathes an air of expectation. The dominant thought is the hope that, out of the future, God will come with his salvation. We shall hear this theme of promise again and again. But we shall also notice that the future is decisive for human lives right now. It is the coming of God that shapes the present.

This means that the Advent faith is not concerned with making speculative calculations about times and seasons, but it is about the belief that something new is coming in the saving work of God. It is the faith that there are truly new possibilities for the world. But if that is so, then the present is bound to be lived out very differently from what it might have been. If the future were simply to be a continuation of the past as is the present, then life and hope would simply be ordinary. But, if God is coming to save us . . .

This is one reason why we shall encounter a strong moral challenge in the Advent readings. We are not called as Christians to be conformed to this world but to be part of the transformation which is the work of God. The Christian faith affirms that God's salvation is already at work in history, particularly in Jesus. We are called to live out that hope now, in the light of God's coming.

This is why, although we shall find strange and frightening images in the Bible readings, Christians receive the Advent message as one of great joy. The end of the world is not to be found in natural or nuclear disaster but in the coming of God, completing what is already begun in creation and focused in Jesus. So, while many people today view the end of the world in terms of disaster, for Christians it is the very best thing that could happen.

Waiting is a feature of all living. The British have almost made an art form of it in queuing! We wait for news, for examination results, for the baby, for the post. You might say that the important question of life is, 'For whom or for what are you waiting?', because whoever or whatever it is dominates your life. Advent both raises that question and proclaims a truly liberating answer. It announces the coming of God at Christmas and at the end of time. No wonder it is the season of hope! We need to pause in the Christmas rush in order to hear its good news.

Living through Advent

What follows in this book are four chapters, each one given over to an Advent week. Each chapter briefly introduces the theme and then comments on the lectionary readings. These are from the Church of England's *Alternative Service Book* – the most commonly-used lectionary in Protestant churches in England. It is vital, therefore, that you read through each reading from the Bible before looking at the comments. The aim of all this is to help us **hear** the Advent message in the Bible. To conclude each chapter, there are some personal reflections on the main themes.

It makes sense then to take each chapter week by week during Advent. It is possible to use this book with a group and to that end some discussion questions are included. There are also suggestions for things to do in families or as individuals as part of your Advent preparation for Christmas.

This introductory chapter concludes with suggestions for church worship and home life. Many churches mark Advent Sundays with an Advent wreath of four candles. Each week a candle is lit and the main Bible reading is read while the whole congregation, young and old, is together. Sometimes a group might be asked to lead the worship at this point with a child lighting the candle, a young person reading the lesson and an adult leading the prayer. In such simple actions the church is helped to follow through the Advent season.

Some churches celebrate with an Advent carol service on the first of the four Sundays. On these occasions the strong Advent hymns can be sung while the choice of readings introduces the whole church to the Advent themes.

But why not have Advent candles at home? Make your own Advent ring and place it on the table at the main meals during the four weeks. As in church, light the appropriate number of candles, and then say *Grace*. Some families share a Bible reading at the table, or even sing a chorus or hymn together. Family worship is not so familiar among Christians as once it was. Advent might be a time for imaginative experiments. Some of the suggestions made at the end of the following chapters might even be taken up for discussion at mealtimes together. Many a home still has an Advent calendar. Perhaps you could make your own with a greater Christian emphasis than the usual commercial ones.

Advent is an important time for Christians. It begins the Christian year, even if it does so by concentrating on 'the last things'. Let us pray to God that we shall learn and live its lessons in preparation for Christmas and until he comes.

A prayer

Living God, beginning and end, always present, always coming, open our minds to understand the message of Advent, open our eyes to recognise your presence with us, open our lips to tell of the hope you give to your people, and open our hearts for the **adven**ture of your ways with us, through Jesus Christ our Lord. Amen.

Some questions and suggestions for further thought

1 What have been the most memorable features of Advent weeks in your own experience?

2 Make a list of questions about Advent and its themes which you hope this book will deal with.

3 If you are reading this book on your own, would it be possible for you to call a small group together to discuss its contents?

4 Have any ideas for Advent come to your mind which you could suggest to your minister, or use at home? Follow them up.

2
Hurting and hoping

The readings for the first Sunday in Advent contain two themes which we must try to hold together – **hurting** and **hoping**. Often enough the situation of God's people is pictured as one of pain or persecution, but within it we hear a message of hope. Suffering is borne, but a word of salvation is also heard. Judgement is taking place, but not without joy. In holding these elements together lies much of the secret of appreciating the message of the Bible readings in this chapter.

We are already preparing for Christmas. In that light some of these readings will strike us as very strange. We must remember that Advent includes preparation for the coming of Christ in the past and – to use a phrase we shall not find in the Bible – his second coming. What is the relationship between these two?

Both stress the initiative of God; both 'comings' involve judgement. They are about salvation and recognise that the existing order of things is going to be disturbed. We have to take that thought quite seriously. Much of the Christianity we know and practise leaves a great deal of our lives and the life of the world as it is. Christians can be very conventional people; but Christmas and the promise of Christ's coming again are properly disturbing. It is as if God is saying that what things have become, and how they are, is not what he intended and hoped for. He is coming and the purpose of his coming is to save us from what we are and what we are making of his world.

In this sense both the message of Advent and Christmas is subversive of all evil schemes and policies. It is a challenging message – socially, politically, economically, ecologically and, not least, religiously. In other words, we must be ready to be disturbed. We may not find the comfort of the first Sunday of Advent very comfortable at all.

New possibilities for old failures   Isaiah 51.4 – 11

Four of the Old Testament readings in Advent come from a part of **Isaiah** which Bible scholars often refer to as *Deutero*, or *Second*, **Isaiah**. Because it is always important to think about a Bible reading in its own historical context it is worth while spending a little time discovering why we talk of more than one Isaiah.

In the Old Testament, the book of **Isaiah** appears as a single text; but, in fact, it comes from different times in Israel's history. For example, chapters 1 – 39 belong to the eighth century before Christ. Isaiah of Jerusalem was a near contemporary of Amos, Hosea, and Micah, at a time when Judah's social immorality and empty religiosity meant that national failure and defeat was drawing ever nearer. That defeat came when Nebuchadnezzar of Babylon overwhelmed Israel in 597 BC and many leading citizens were deported to exile. Then, ten years later, in another assault of devastating consequence, Jerusalem itself was destroyed.

The days of exile in Babylon were full of humiliation. The Jews lived there suffering all those heavy experiences of discrimination that go with being a minority group. **Isaiah 40 – 55** belongs to the time of exile up to 562 BC, the date of the death of Nebuchadnezzar. During their years in Babylon many of the Jews had built their own homes. They traded as craftsmen and bankers, and began to take their own religion and covenant identity seriously again. Jeremiah 29.4 – 7 is one prophet's message telling the Jews that the days of exile would be long and the people must not think of an early return home. But, with the death of Nebuchadnezzar, there inevitably arose some hope of a new life. However, this was not to be. **Isaiah 56 – 66** belongs to the period of internal strike and uncertainty in Babylon, during which the exiles had to bear more than their share of pain. Eventually, in 539 BC, Cyrus of Persia defeated the Babylonians. Within a year he had passed an edict which allowed the Israelites to return home to rebuild Jerusalem and its temple (2 Chronicles 36.22 – 23; Ezra 1.1 – 4).

So, when we listen to Bible readings from Isaiah 40 – 55, we need to think of a people far away from home, humiliated, whose faith in God had taken a hard knock but who, through the prophet, were hearing a message of hope. The days in Babylon had caused them to think once again of God, of their calling to be God's people, of the reality of judgement as part of, and not in spite of, God's covenant love.

Read Isaiah 51.4 – 11 again, slowly. Notice the imperatives, 'Listen to me . . .', 'Hearken to me . . .', in verses 4 and 7. This is God speaking to the exiles through his messenger.

In verses 4 – 6 the promise of God's purposes for his people and all the nations of the world is affirmed. God's teaching, his justice, his work of liberation, is to be for everybody. The days of waiting in hope will come to fruition in God's plans for a new world. This came as a remarkable word of reassurance after all the days of disaster and disappointment. Here is the picture of God who brings new possibilities out of old failures. God's deliverance is said to be something that 'will be for ever' (verse 6). The victory he brings will be final. When the foundations are really shaken and the end of everything seems to be upon us – as the Advent message proclaims – God remains the one security.

Verses 7 – 8 are addressed to the people of God. They are not to be afraid, certainly not afraid of those who abuse and pour scorn on them in their apparent weakness. They may be harassed and humiliated, but God's deliverance is coming!

In verses 9 – 11 it is God who is addressed by the people. Out of their desperation they call on God to stir himself. They want God to act, and the basis of their hope is what he has done in the past. Very significantly both creation and liberation are mentioned together. Verse 9, with its reference to Rahab, the monster of the original deep chaotic waters, takes up the mighty acts of creation. Just as God struggled there to bring his purposes to birth, now he is called upon to struggle again. Then, in verse 10, the exodus is recalled, when the people were liberated from slavery and set out on the journey to the land of promise.

In Babylon, these two great affirmations of the labours in creation and the crossing of the Red Sea are recalled together to proclaim a new work of God – he will bring his people back to Jerusalem for a new beginning in joy and gladness. It is as if the one process of God's saving work is still continuing. These things are happening in real history because God is at work – in judgement and liberation. He is going to bring his people home; that is the good news. Just as he brought his people to life in creation and exodus, so new possibilities are hardly beyond him in Babylon. Therefore, the whole attitude of the people of God is to be one of hope and not despair.

God is good news   Isaiah 52.7 – 10

These verses are ones that people, rightly, have always wanted to sing. The people of Israel may have had all kinds of reasons for not singing the Lord's song in the strange cruel world of exile (see Psalm 137); but now the tears of bitter anguish could give way to shouts of joy. Our God reigns!

The picture is of a messenger coming back to Jerusalem, weaving his way between the hills. Over the mountains he comes and his message is one of the greatest possible encouragement. It is the good news of God, who has triumphed over the seemingly irresistible power of Babylon. What people had thought were ultimate limitations turn out not to be so at all. For the truth is that God has been working out his purpose all along. He, too, has gone into exile, sharing in the suffering and disgrace of his people. Now he comes in triumph.

Everyone can see the truth of the situation. God and his people are coming back to Zion – Jerusalem. The messenger proclaims it. The watchmen keeping guard over the waste places of the city take up the cry. And, in the end, all Jerusalem will join in the song celebrating such amazing and unexpected news.

It is not, of course, the actual return that the prophet is describing. He is delivering the all-important message that the King is coming. God has set out. He is on his way. Who knows how long this journey will take? The important point, however, is that he is coming. That is the truth of the matter and everything must now be seen in that light. Life is to be lived in the knowledge that, out of the future, the Saviour is coming.

In all this it could be seen that God was somehow

being vindicated. In the ancient world people used to think of a god and his people, as inseparably linked together. Success, or defeat, of a nation was regarded as success, or defeat, for that nation's god. The implication of the exile was that the God of Judah was not as strong and powerful as the gods of Babylon. But now, after the days of exile, God will come again to show that his purposes, although apparently weak and vulnerable, are the ones that matter in the end. Amazingly God has allowed himself to know humiliation with his people to go into exile and captivity before the mocking eyes of the nations. He had not forgotten nor ignored his people, much as it must have looked like that at times. He has borne with them the disgrace and punishment that inevitably followed on their sin. Who would ever have thought of a god like that? But Israel and the nations now know that God is faithful. He even shares his people's hurt and pain.

Are you ready? 1 Thessalonians 5.1–11

Readings such as these give us the sense of entering into an unusual and very unfamiliar world. To hear their message and understand it, takes some imagination and thought. But things can be both strange and true.

When we read 1 Thessalonians we are looking at one of the oldest documents of the New Testament – a letter from Paul written about twenty years after Jesus' death and resurrection. In 1 Thessalonians 5.1–11 we read something of Paul's teaching on a fundamental tenet of early Christian belief – the coming again of Jesus Christ. Try to imagine what it must be like to live with the thought that today, tomorrow, certainly very soon now, all human history will have run its course and

God's work of salvation will be complete as Christ comes as Lord. We say in the *Creeds* that we believe that Christ will come again to be our judge. But the first Christians really thought that would happen soon. Paul seems to have thought that Christ would come in his own lifetime (see 1 Corinthians 15.51 – 52).

This sense of the end was part of the spirit of the age. Not only Christians, but other religious believers as well, thought they were living in the last days. Some people responded to that by being quite irresponsible. They did not go to work, nor did they care much about what was happening around them. Why should they if it was all going to end soon?

What was important for the early Christians was not that the end was coming but that Christ was coming. The Old Testament concept of the Day of the Lord, with all its themes of God's vindication of his purposes and the enactments of his judgement, was thought of by Paul and others as the Day of Christ (see Acts 17.31; 1 Corinthians 5.5; 2 Peter 3.10).

Had not Jesus spoken of the suddenness of the coming (see Luke 21.34 – 36)? His emphasis was on the importance of being prepared because his coming would be sudden and not announced. Every moment has its own urgency. The day would come, but it would not be entirely out of the blue for Christians. They, above all, ought not to be caught unawares because this day, although it will not be without its pain and terror, is the one to which Christians can look forward. Christians live in hope of Christ's coming when God's work of salvation will be consummated.

So the Advent hope includes an obligation to live the Christian life now, in faith, love and hope (verse 8), Christians show that faith precisely by responsible living. Jesus said, 'Blessed are those servants whom the

27

master finds awake when he comes' (Luke 12.37a). So let us watch and pray, and encourage one another in living this faith. The coming of Christ in the near future is no excuse for abandoning responsibilities now. Indeed, it simply underlines the need to live the life in Christ.

What we have to admit is that, in terms of time-scale, those early convictions were mistaken. Christ did not return quickly and there is evidence in the New Testament itself for a reappraisal of how the belief in his coming was to be expressed.

But hope was not abandoned. Nor could it be. It was an expression of Christian faith in the fulfilment of all God's purposes revealed in Christ. The kingdom that we pray for will come because the King will come. The sense of timing of the first Christians might have been wrong but not the faith, nor the urgent call to responsible dedicated commitment to Christ and his cause. Perhaps, as F F Bruce suggests, we in our time have to realise that constantly, urgently, it is not so much an event as a Person who is near. Each day is the day of his coming to us, until he finally comes. We have hope because God has already set out on the coming journey of our salvation!

Salvation is coming nearer   Romans 13.8 – 14

Perhaps you can recall the experience, as a small child, of being told for the first time that you are going on holiday to the seaside. From that moment on all the world was charged with excitement. Parents quickly learn not to give this information too far ahead to young children, otherwise there will be no escape from the seemingly perpetual question, 'Are we going soon?'

The promise and expectation of the coming holiday is the context in which the whole life of the child is lived. It is the first thing that friends and visitors are told because the coming holiday is never far from the child's mind. There may be temporary diversions, but irresistibly it seems mind and imagination are brought back to the promise of what is to come.

So, for Paul, the context of his life and of all human life is the new age. Already, into human history, there has come God's important saving work in Jesus Christ. God's work of salvation in the cross and resurrection has already taken place and a new age in the human story has been inaugurated. What is happening now, in Paul's mind, is the living out of the last days.

Paul pictures Christians as people who have seen the sunrise at the dawn of the day. Others may still be asleep, dull to the wonder of what is happening, unaware of the time. But Christians have awoken, or rather been awakened, to all this. Paul uses this analogy to make important points about Christian living now. The fact that our salvation is nearer now, and coming nearer, is the context of his moral teaching. Christians are called upon to obey the command to love because they know the significance of the time. Paul understands that Christian living will not be without struggle. He talks about armour (or weapons). Putting aside our fallen human nature is no easy matter. But the Christian's calling is to live the life in Christ. This is the day to do just that. Let us live out the implications of our baptism, because the great day of salvation is nearer than it was.

Watch, pray and hope   Luke 21.25 – 33

What are we to make of these words? Hopefully, a little

29

background knowledge will help us to understand them.

In the Old Testament there are verses that appear to point forward to a time in Israel's life when God will send an important new leader, of the house of David, through whom God's purposes for the nation and all the nations of the earth will be fulfilled. In his coming and his rule there will be a new age.

In the time between the Old and New Testaments there appeared forms of writing which expressed this hope often in vivid and dramatic language. This kind of language is called *'apocalyptic'*, from a Greek word which means to uncover, disclose or reveal. We have already seen how the early Christians took up the notion of the Day of the Lord and related it to the return of Jesus Christ. We know that that return was expected.

One feature of apocalyptic language was its emphasis on persecutions and the inevitable sufferings for God's people. More than that, the imagery was often of terrors, disturbances and catastrophic events which were tantamount to the very foundations of creation being shaken. Like any new birth, the coming of the new age was painful.

One other things we must note by way of background. There is good evidence to suggest that Jesus gave warning of the destruction of the temple in Jerusalem. Luke's Gospel was written after the Jewish war which ended in AD 70 and brought a catastrophic end to Jerusalem and its holy temple. It would hardly be surprising if many, especially Christians, did not see these events as precisely one of those signs of the end and the coming of the Lord. Luke, like all of the Gospel writers, was concerned not only to tell the story of Jesus but to do so in conscious recognition of the needs and circumstances of the Church of his day.

Luke does indeed seem to see these social, religious and political events as signs of the new age, its dawning and presence. He calls on Christians to be vigilant and watchful. Like Paul, he affirms that 'your redemption (salvation) is drawing near' (verse 28); and he does not mean by this some personal individual salvation but an event of cosmic significance brought about by God. So let Christians keep their heads up. Let them remain true to their calling, and hopeful, because it is Christ who comes. The reading ends on a great word of hope. The earth and all human life with its institutions may be shaken to their very core, but the word and promises of God will abide sure for ever. That is the kind of hope Christians have. It is, above all, hope in the purposes of the Christlike God.

When the Son of Man comes   Matthew 25.31 – 46

We have all grown used to hearing this described as the parable of the sheep and goats, or of the last judgement, and many preachers have taken the 'as you did it to the least of these my brethren . . .' as a challenge to us to care for the hungry, thirsty, naked, sick, strangers, prisoners and all others in need. We have heard a call for a caring, humanitarian mission in response to Jesus who identifies himself with the poor. All this is very important and significant, but let us look at a different emphasis, studying the text rather more closely with the help of the kind of insights which come from New Testament scholars.

First, let us note the theme of separation. It is one that is present in other teachings of Jesus (see Matthew 13.24 – 30, 47 – 50). A shepherd in Israel would take care, when evening came, to separate any sheep and goats which had grazed together through the day but needed different attention for the cold night hours. With the idea of separation we have the theme of judgement. The writer of Matthew's Gospel uses apocalyptic imagery in chapter 25 to heighten the sense of the coming God. Since the shepherd image is related to that of the king, which in turn is related to God, we have, indeed, an allegory of the last judgement.

But what is the basis of the separation? Is it whether or not we have responded to human need with humanitarian acts? If so, then salvation is a matter of 'works' and God will decide among us on the basis of our performance. His coming will not be to save us so much as to examine us. But this interpretation alone does not fit in well with the rest of Jesus' teaching about the kingdom and the early Church's hope of salvation as being a work of God.

Who are the 'least of these my brethren'? In Matthew's Gospel 'brethren' means 'disciples'. Therefore, the reading may be suggesting that the issue is whether or not the servants of the king and their message have been accepted and received. Thus these verses are about response to Jesus and to the message about him which is now being proclaimed by his disciples.

Verse 32 says that 'all the nations' will be gathered for judgement, although what follows implies response not to nations but to individual persons. Is the Gospel writer saying that the Gentiles, the peoples of the nations, may not directly have encountered Christ but that he has been present among them in the form of the 'brethren' – his own messengers? If so, then the crucial question is about response to Jesus, his message, and God's saving action in and through him. The contrast is not between those who showed compassion to Christians and those who did not, but between Gentiles who serve Christ without knowing or recognising him and Christians who call Jesus, 'Lord', but do not serve him in the persons of suffering and vulnerable fellow Christians. As Jesus said in the Sermon on the Mount, 'Not everyone who says to me, "Lord, Lord," shall enter the kingdom of heaven' (Matthew 7.21).

Looked at in this way, the reading may then be heard as a serious warning to Christians. Simply to profess Christ with the lips is no guarantee of salvation. When the judgement comes a more searching light will be shone. All will be brought to judgement. This part of Matthew's Gospel discourages us from relying only upon our **works** or upon our **faith**. What matters is: Who, or what, are we living for? Jesus has been calling everyone to see the works of the kingdom already present. Will we allow our eyes to be open? Will we have God to rule over us? He may come to us anonymously but he is undoubtedly present and coming.

Some personal reflections

The Bible readings will have prompted all kinds of reflections in our minds. The paragraphs that conclude this chapter are not offered as an exhaustive account of what the readings mean. Rather, they are only some personal reflections on the questions and affirmations of faith.

First, we have had to recognise the strangeness in some of the language and ideas in these readings. It is difficult to enter into a sense of anticipation that the end of the world may come at any moment when history is completed in the coming of Christ. Two kinds of difficulties face us here.

In the first place, history did not end as some early Christians seem to have believed it would. Jesus Christ did not come back within their lifetime as they implied. They were wrong. There is no point in saying otherwise. But that is not to say that they were wrong in faith, only in their chronological sense of history. The years have gone on and still Christ has not returned in the literal manner the texts suggest. We must leave it there. It is not the first, nor will it be the last, time that Christians have been mistaken in detailed aspects of what they believe. We are human, after all. We see through a glass darkly. To make this confession is not to belittle Scripture; it is to recognise its humanity.

A second difficulty is more practical. Christians proclaim that Christ will come again. We may not be literalistic about those Advent readings but we do affirm the faith they affirm. Fundamentally, that faith is faith in God, the Lord of history. Our personal life and that of all creation is lived out in that divine context. The cosmos and its history is not aimless and senseless. One day, all the purposes of God will be brought to completion.

The first Christians lived with the thought of God's imminent coming. This conviction helped to shape all their living, influencing the responses they made in home, marriage, employment – in fact, in every part of life. That conviction remains as an important challenge to us: How shall we live our lives seriously, consciously, responsibly and hopefully in the time before the coming of God, that is, the God known to us in Jesus?

◊ The six readings all remind us that the gospel is the good news of **God**. The heart of the Advent messages is the coming of **God**. It could not have been straightforward for the people of Israel to keep their faith in God during the years of the exile. It could not have been easy to live out the Christian life in the early days of the Church. But their faith was in the faithful, coming, liberating God. It was the faith which affirmed that not only at the end of history but even now God is working out his purposes in his own way. The challenge of faith in **God** is the challenge at the heart of our Christian faith. We may forget this as we hear so many sermons about the Church, evangelism, ministry or other ecclesiastical concerns. But the good news is the good news of **God**.

The God of the Bible is the One who is ever working to bring new possibilities out of present and past failures. If we believe that God will do unpredictable, saving things in the future, we can also assert that he may surprise us in his action now. The story of the exile and the return tells of God's willingness and desire to leave no situation beyond his redeeming work. There is no washing of the divine hands when the world is in need. God remains ever active to bring about his salvation. The question is: How?

◊ To answer a question like that we must keep as close to God's coming in Jesus as we can. When we do, we cannot but notice the vulnerability of the baby Jesus, immediately at risk from Herod and the power struggles of the day. A shadow of the cross falls across the Bethlehem cradle. God's way of redemption involves being with his people in their suffering and disgrace, and bringing from it all new beginnings and renewal of hope. One of the amazing insights of Israel

35

during the humiliating years of exile was that God shared all that with his people. He was disgraced among the nations; his name was dishonoured. Yet he kept covenant; and, out of the disaster, brought new possibilities and new knowledge of his love.

How much more is this so in Jesus! From the cradle to the cross God's way is one of vulnerable shame-bearing love. His kingdom is not advanced by brute force, nor coercion, nor by his pulling rank. His presence among us is never without pain – for him and for his people. He is the giver of new hope and life. But no birth is painless, not even for God.

What about judgement? We could not help but notice this theme coming through in the readings. Sometimes judgement was emphasised as a feature of the end of history. At other times, God was working out his judgement in history, in the social, political and national events of the time.

How shall we think of God's judgement? It is not a popular theme, but we have seen that it is central to the Advent message. Clearly the Bible writers saw the seriousness of sin before God. The law of God could not be flouted as if it were a matter of no great consequence. No more could Israel, Judah or anyone else presume upon God's mercy, as if unrighteousness and injustice could be so easily overlooked. God will be our Judge, but his judgement will not be made apart from his mercy and love for us.

This is a theme we shall take up again more thoroughly in the last chapter of this book. Let us just note one implication here, evident in several of the readings, that there is a moral seriousness in the calling of a Christian. There abides the challenge to live responsibly, before God. To live responsibly is to live in faith of the coming God, as those who are of the light, living in the day which even now is beginning to dawn. This means being willing to oppose the evils of our age, such as racism, poverty, sexual discrimination, materialism, and much else in the name and hope of Christ. That is why Christians can, and do, throw in their lot against all manner of injustice in spite of the fact that, humanly speaking, they have little chance of changing the situation at all.

Finally, let us reflect on the two senses in which we speak of an **end**. A ball of string has an end. This day of twenty-four hours will have an end. Every football match will have a final whistle that will signal the end of the game. So **end** can mean the finish of something, a moment of time or measurement.

But there is another meaning of **end** – it is the purpose of something. 'What is the chief end of man?' asks an old confession of faith; and the answer is, 'The chief end of man is to glorify God and enjoy him for ever.' That is what we are here for; that is our purpose, our goal, our reason for being – our **end**.

The Advent readings have spoken at times of the end of history. As such they combine both time and purpose. History will come to an end, but that end is expressed in the coming of Christ, of God's salvation. That is why, although we may not be very optimistic about the state and future of the world, we can live with heads held high and hearts full of hope. The Church lives on, until Christ comes, as a community of both hurt and hope – hurt, by reason of our sin and the sin of the world; but also hope, because we know something of the end. We may not know **when**, but we do know **who** is coming.

A prayer

Loving God, the first and the last and the living One, we acknowledge your claim upon our lives. We thank you that you have kept faith with us, borne with us, even in our shame and disobedience. Your suffering, patient love knows no defeat. So, in gratitude and wonder, we offer you our living in this Advent season and we worship you, our Judge, our Saviour and our hope, through Jesus Christ our Lord. Amen.

Some questions and suggestions for further thought

1 We have enough nuclear weaponry to extinguish all life on earth. What do you think it means for a Christian to live faithfully in this situation?

2 The people described in the parable of the sheep and the goats in Matthew 25.31–46 were all, in different ways, in situations where hope was in short supply. Think of such people today. What would it mean for us to help them to have hope? What action can we take?

3 The two readings from Isaiah (51.4–11 and 52.7–10) came from a time when Israel was in exile. Find out – from your local branch of Amnesty International or elsewhere – about some people who are in exile today. Perhaps you could send a special Christmas greeting to one of them.

4 The God of the Bible is one who can bring new hope and life out of the most unpromising situations. Does this ring true in your own experience or that of anyone you know?

3
Listening for the word

Dietrich Bonhoeffer in his book, *Life Together*, which contains beautiful and helpful thoughts for his students on the meaning of community, emphasised the importance of listening. Christians, he remarked, are frequently tempted to think that they must always be speaking; but, in fact, listening is often the greater service we can pay one another. Ours is a very noisy age, full of words and sounds. All of us too readily contribute to that cacophony. What we do not do is listen carefully enough. We know how frustrating it is to speak and not be heard because our 'listeners' are too preoccupied with what they are going to say next. They do not hear because they want to speak.

When we are not listening to one another, then any kind of community life fails. This is true in a family. Teenagers do not always want to talk with their parents, but when they do they want to be taken seriously. They need their parents to listen – or else relationships will begin to fracture. We encourage and support the elderly by sitting and listening to their reminiscences. We need to listen to one another in Church, otherwise our fellowship will become empty. We can only deal creatively with conflict when we take care to hear what is actually being said. A fellowship of believers is not created by monologue or some aimless competition with those who can shout the loudest.

Bonhoeffer called on his students to learn to listen to one another. There is an important rule of the spiritual life here because, as Bonhoeffer argued, whoever does not bother to listen to other people will soon not be listening to God either. Rather than paying attention there will be the chatter of empty phrases, platitudes and cheap patronising noises. We do too much of this in the Church – and they did too much of it in ancient Israel.

The readings for the second Sunday in Advent can be seen as having the one theme, that of the **word of God**. Whom are we listening for? Are we listening at all? How does God speak his word? Have we already decided what he is going to say? Maybe we go on chattering because we sense there may be a risk in our saying, 'Speak, Lord, your servant is listening.' In many churches, the second Sunday in Advent is also known as Bible Sunday.

The promise of God's word   Isaiah 55.1 – 11

Christians sometimes read this lesson, not only in Advent but on the Saturday before Easter Sunday. That is not to be wondered at. It certainly conveys the air of something remarkable about to happen. It is like standing poised on the brink. The people are about to return to Jerusalem. The days of exile are coming to an end and hopes are running high. Perhaps they dreamt of making the nation great again, restoring the royal house of David to its former authority and splendour. That would be understandable enough. But God, speaking through his messenger, has something else in mind.

Isaiah 55 begins with an invitation. Before, the people set their hearts on transitory, unsatisfying desires and hoped for goals that were partial, temporary and unfulfilling. Now, they are called to hear what God has to say and give to them for their well-being and nourishment.

The God they know is one who covenants with his people, as he did with David. What they are to remember is God's covenant with David, not David himself. By making and keeping covenant God works to fulfil his purposes not just for Israel but, through them, for all the nations of the earth. Israel must realise that God's mission through his covenant people is more important than dreams about the dynasty of David. That dynasty may have ended but God's covenant calling of Israel has not ended. Let the people find their hope in God and listen to his words, then they will have life (verse 3).

Israel has not been true to her calling. Hence, the humiliation of exile for her people and for God. She sought privilege without responsibility. Now, in Babylon, she hears again of her glory which is to participate in God's mission to all the nations. Before she hurries home, full of her own ideas, she must listen to God.

God issues a great call for repentance (verses 6–7). The people must turn again to him **now**. There is an urgency about this moment, as they stand on the brink of new possibilities. Their minds are full of all manner of hopes and dreams, but God's thoughts are different from theirs (verse 8). Now is the time to turn again, to bend mind and purpose to God's will. Part of their failure in the past was their unwillingness to listen. They assumed that God shared and approved of their desires. But the truth is that the people of God always presume too much here. They identify God's will with their desires. But God is not simply Israel – or any group of humans – on a large scale.

So the call is to repent, to turn again to God their Lord

and liberator. And the reading ends with a great promise – that God's word will accomplish his purpose. One of the differences between all humans and God is that of the many, many words we speak, sing or write, only a very few have any real effect. But with God, his word, his will, his purpose is always achieved. When God speaks, things happen.

Remember the way the Bible begins, with God saying, 'Let there be light' (Genesis 1.3). The result of the word was light! So the Bible sees the closest connection between God's word and God's deeds enacted. Here, in Isaiah 55, the promise of God's word is being addressed to a world of need. It is, as ever, an effective word. It makes for life. Even as the snow and rain come upon the earth to water it and make the crops grow, producing grain for food and seed for next year's sowing, so God's word will enter into the life of the nation when the people turn to him. There the word will bring new life to light, open up new possibilities and real changes will be made. Israel has God's promise.

The cry of the desperate   Isaiah 64.1–7

There is a deep cry of desperation here. Technically this reading is part of what scholars call a 'community lament'. Some say the context is that of those frustrating days as the people of Israel wait to return to their own land. Others claim that the setting is after the return, when the people are back in Jerusalem. However, nothing much has changed, the temple is in ruins and all their high hopes have been brought down to earth with a bump.

Certainly, whatever the precise context out of which the reading comes, the people express an attitude with which many Christians can identify. God's people are trying to come to terms with their very confusing experience. They know they are not orphans (see Isaiah 63.16 and 64.8), but they do feel themselves abandoned. They appeal to God to come and put things right. The language they use (verses 1–4) is that of an 'epiphany' – a moment of God's appearing. They recall the other times when God's presence was known among them, taking them by surprise as the world about them had its foundations shaken.

They confess their sin, admitting their continued failure to live as God's people and they even acknowledge that their best deeds do not amount to much before God. In spite of the knowledge of God's anger against them, they have persisted in working against his will. They recognise that it is their sin that has led to their present confusion and disorientation. They know that they do not even turn properly to God – no one goes to God for help (verse 7). God is hidden from them; they feel abandoned in their sin.

The reading is the deep lament of a people who know and recognise their failure. God cannot be blamed for their state; yet, they know that their only hope and future is with him. This comes over even more strongly if you read the whole of Isaiah 63.15 – 64.12. The Advent hope is expressed in the context of the people's helplessness and their feelings of abandonment which have come upon them because of their own tragic waywardness. Yet, they have not forgotten their true identity. They call for God.

Being kept in the faith 2 Timothy 3.14 – 4.5

It is no surprise that this reading should appear on Bible

Sunday. The reference to 'Holy Scriptures' or 'sacred writings' (verse 15) is probably to the Old Testament, but the notion of inspired Scripture certainly extends to the New Testament as far as Christians are concerned.

The Pastoral Epistles – 1, 2 Timothy and Titus – are among the latest of the New Testament documents to have been written. Already, it seems, the faith was being distorted and all kinds of myths or legends (verse 4) were being substituted for the gospel message. Perhaps, because these stories were less demanding, and therefore popular, they were being preached by those who had been wandering from the apostolic faith. It is always a temptation for any preacher to give people what they want to hear.

The charge to Timothy is to remain true to the faith he has received from his own mother and grandmother, and from the Scriptures. This was the foundation for his life of faith. What foundation? The question is pressing because the New Testament itself shows that there never was one finished form in which the faith of the Church was expressed. From the very first, there was a genuine diversity of Christian experience and understanding in the early Church. But, at the heart of it all, there is the one foundation of Jesus Christ to which the apostles and the Scriptures bear witness. He may be interpreted in different ways but he is the One on whom it all depends. Any proclamation that directly denies him is not to be trusted (1 John 4.2 – 3).

Discharging a Christian ministry means proclaiming and exalting Jesus Christ. The importance of the Scriptures is in helping us to identify who he is. Many may come announcing the end of the world – the day of judgement – even saying that they are the Christ. But the One who is to come is the One who has come. The Scriptures will keep Timothy and all other readers in the faith, with their lives centred on Christ. Preachers may be tempted to offer other possibilities which seem attractive, especially when the going gets hard and faith is under trial. But we are called to preach the good news of the One who came, is present and is yet to come, and who calls us to costly discipleship.

The God of all hope   Romans 15.4 – 13

Bishop Lesslie Newbigin used to be a missionary in India. He lived there for a number of years until he returned to Britain. One of the things that struck him most forcibly on his return was the general air of hope-lessness in the lives of far too many British people. Whether it was rising unemployment, increasing poverty, or a depressingly heavy blanket of secularism, it seemed to have dulled people's eyes and weighed down their spirits.

To be without hope is, in an important sense, to be disabled. If you have no hope, you have no future. That means you have no surprises before you. You expect everything to remain as it is at present. So life is dull; it is boring. There is nothing worth giving thanks for because the good life is in the past – the rest is hopeless.

In contrast with such a dismal prospect, Paul writes to the Romans about the Christian life as being a life filled with hope. There may be those who think their lives have run into a cul-de-sac, or are simply heading to a dead end, but Christian living is not like this. The Christian view of life is one that looks forward because there is much to look forward to.

Paul affirms in these verses that the Scriptures were written in order that we might have hope. The

Scriptures themselves are not the source of hope, but they bear witness that God is the source of all hope.

This is a very important theological affirmation. God is the God **of hope**. If there were no God, there would be no surprises, no new creation. Hope is not the same as optimism. Optimism is a humanly-grounded conviction that it will be all right – that something will turn up – because life is like that. Hope is different. For Christians, it is believing that into every situation there comes the One who has power to make new, to surprise and awaken us. The future is a gift which God brings. It is space into which we can move.

The Scriptures tell us of this ever-creating, ever-renewing, ever-surprising God of hope. Christians are sometimes criticised for being backward-looking people. It is true that much of our services of worship and many Scripture readings tell of God long ago doing wonderful things and surprising his people. However, we read these stories precisely because, on the basis of this activity of God in the past, we may have hope for the future. It is out of the future that God will come, creating space and room for us to live. God is the source of all hope. Paul sees this in dynamic terms. By the power of the Holy Spirit our hope may continue to grow.

One last thought on this reading: God is spoken of as the source of hope. But does God have his hopes? In the coming of Jesus we hear the proclamation of the kingly rule of God. We learn of God's will to save, his searching for the lost and his waiting like a parent for the return of children who have lost their way. God has his hopes for the world. If he should give up on them, or on us, then we are hopeless indeed. God is the source of all hope because he is himself the God of hope.

Only God can reveal God   John 5.36b – 47

History is full of those who have come claiming to speak for God, or even to be God! However do we assess such claims? Where would we go for an answer? Has anyone actually ever seen God?

Any conclusion we come to must inevitably be one of faith. God is not a part of the world and therefore open to our inspection, exploration and proof. He cannot be dug up, or fed through a computer, or put under a microscope. To think in these terms at all is to misunderstand God. He is **other** than we are, in a category of his own that is beyond our knowledge and skill to define exhaustively. God, as God, is always **beyond** us. If this were not so, then God would not be God. Thus even our best theories and our most perceptive ways of talking about God only approximate to the truth.

All of this is coming at the question from our end. Is it possible for God to reveal and authenticate himself? The Christian faith affirms that he does. So who is God? And how will he be recognised?

John's Gospel proclaims that Jesus, the prophet from Nazareth, is the Word made flesh (1.14). Here is God in his self-revelation. The writer of the Fourth Gospel knows that no one has ever seen God. But has he made himself known? The answer is 'Yes'. God reveals himself in his own way and this certainly conflicts with the expectations of Jesus' contemporaries.

The religious leaders of the day reject Jesus. He brings healing to a paralysed man, but he does this on the Sabbath. This is but one of a number of events which make the Jews so agitated that they are determined to kill him (John 5.18). So far as they are concerned Jesus does not reveal God; rather, he is an offence to God. 'Who does he think he is' sums up their attitude.

These verses are only a small part of a long chapter on the theme of Jesus' authority and status. The point is that only God can authenticate God. Has God, in fact, given that authentication?

John 5 as a whole indicates three 'witnesses' concerning who Jesus really is. The first is John the Baptist (verses 33 – 35). Then there are the deeds Jesus has performed, deeds that are not done on his own behalf, but indicate whose authority he is under (verses 36 – 38). And the third witness is the Scriptures (verse 39). The Jewish leaders studied the *Torah* deeply. One of the sayings of the rabbis put it, 'He who has acquired the word of the *Torah* has acquired eternal life.'

The first two witnesses have been rejected by the leaders: John's testimony is refused, and the works Jesus performs are not seen as signs of his true identity at all. The Scriptures are even more misunderstood because these earnest readers have believed that it is in these words there is eternal life. Yet, they do not believe in the living Word – Jesus Christ. Because of the presuppositions about God which these Jews bring to their reading of the Scriptures, they make the mistake of all those who see the signpost and believe they have come to journey's end.

Why are these witnesses not received? One reason is that the Jews look for someone who will have the praise and glory of human recognition, the sort of thing they give to one another and hopefully expect for themselves. But Jesus does not seek to be someone! He does not appear to want to make anything of himself at all. So he is not significant in their eyes. But the truth, as John's Gospel proclaims, is that it is precisely because he does not respond in their way by seeking acclaim and glory for himself, that he is the One in and through whom God manifests his glory. Who would have thought of the Son of God with a towel and a basin (John 13.3–5)? Who would have thought of a suffering-servant God? If we look only in the realm of our own expectations and standards we shall miss the divine presence in Jesus because in our terms he claims nothing at all for himself.

These witnesses do not 'prove' the authority of the claim of Jesus – they point to who he is. The truth of the claim will only be known in the following – in the active practice of discipleship. The tragedy for Jesus' contemporaries was, for example in the case of the Scriptures, that they could not see beyond their all too human presuppositions. They deified their interpretation and so missed the divine presence. Do we do the same with the Scripture, our preachers, our churches, our ways of thinking about God? Do we miss the coming of God because God does not fit in with our expectations?

Scripture comes true   Luke 4.14 – 21

Here Jesus is pictured at the beginning of his ministry, reading and commenting on the meaning of an extract from Scripture, which we know as Isaiah 61.1–2. It is a word of prophecy about one on whom the Spirit of the Lord would come and through whom there would be the announcement in deed and word of the coming messianic age. This Gospel reading is sometimes spoken of as Jesus' manifesto. These verses are full of hope. There is One, chosen by God, who will come with good news, especially for the poor, the prisoners, the blind and the oppressed. To all these, the good news is that the time has come when God will save his people. Jesus said that time is now.

Reading on in Luke 4 we see how people's attitude to Jesus changes. First, it seems to be admiration. The local boy has made good! The congregation in his home town is impressed. Then, when his sermon has gone further, they are not so sure and their doubt eventually turns to anger. Why has he not read on in Isaiah to that part which speaks about the Gentiles really being put in their place (61.5)? He seems to be implying that these foreigners will actually be included in the blessings of the messianic age! So, in anger, they try to do away with this disturber of their peaceful prejudices. People who are very zealous about their personal position and rights are not always ready to listen for the One whose calling includes speaking for the rights of others.

Perhaps this is always the way with the coming of Jesus. At first we are impressed – with the baby in the manger or with the preacher of such high and attractive ideals. Then, we begin to realise a little of what this means. The implications of his beautiful words are very disturbing, even revolutionary. The salvation of which Jesus speaks is dynamic and socially disruptive of the *status quo*. Jesus, as the coming salvation of God, brings challenge and choice. The self-satisfied will not want him. The desperate, poor, handicapped, oppressed and forgotten people will welcome him as good news indeed. Is that why they are called 'blessed' (Luke 6.20 – 23)?

In one church, which I have read about, the congregation end their services of worship by standing together and then carefully and slowly saying, 'The Spirit of the Lord is upon us, because he has chosen us to bring good news to the poor . . .' Their worship is over but their service begins. Having heard that today is the day of God's coming, they go out to live in that faith and truth.

Some personal reflections

Among many possible reflections prompted by these readings, we shall focus attention on the theme of the word of God. That God communicates and speaks his word is a fundamental assumption of the Christian faith. It is hearing and obeying that word that makes for life. Some of the readings in this chapter have made that point negatively – when the people do not listen, then they become weak and sick. Few things can be more important for us than listening for the word of God.

Let us focus our reflections around four questions. Deeply contentious issues are at stake here and Christians have fallen out badly over what counts as proper answers. The answers given below are not the only Christian answers; they are the author's reflections against which readers can test and share their own.

What is the relationship between the word of God and the Bible? For some Christians this is a matter of a one-to-one identity – the Bible is the word of God. But many are uneasy about that simple identification. For one thing the Bible is a very human book. In fact, it is a collection of books written in different styles for varied contexts. Within it there is history, stories, songs and letters. We know that these books did not fall out of the sky ready-made.

We also know that, within the Bible, distinctions are made between different texts and the status that may be ascribed to them. For example, in 1 Corinthians 7.10, Paul gives one instruction that he expects to be obeyed because it is from the Lord. However, in verse 25, when he gives another instruction, he does so more cautiously because he has no clear word from the Lord and admits that he is only giving his opinion. Of course, we can claim that Paul wrote his letters under the inspiration of the Holy Spirit. But it is one thing to say that the writers of the Bible were inspired, and quite another to imply that every word they wrote is from God. Muslims believe that the Koran came directly from God (Allah) through the speech of the prophet Muhammad which was then recorded. Christians do not have that view about the Bible.

But there is a deeper and more theological reason why we do not make a simple indentification of the text of the Bible with the word of God. Within the Bible God's word is conceived of in dynamic terms – his word is also his deed. When he speaks, things happen. And most particularly of all, John's Gospel speaks of Jesus as the Word become flesh (see John 1.14).

The Christian experience is that sometimes, by the activity of God, we hear the divine word through the pages of the Bible. That is not surprising since the focal point of God's self-revelation, his Word, is Jesus, and the Scriptures bear the crucial testimony to him. So it might be expected that, if God were to speak any-where, he would speak through these pages; but that again is a long way from identifying God's word with the text itself.

In the reading from Isaiah 55 which we looked at on pages 40 – 42, the point was made that God's thoughts are not like our thoughts, nor are his ways the same as ours. This is good news. The last thing we want is a God who thinks and acts like us. But, since words are the expression of thoughts, it means that there can be no simple identification between human words and God's word. Yet, in his freedom, God who spoke his Word in Jesus, can and does take up the words of the biblical writers and speaks through them even now.

Where would we expect to hear God's word today?
An answer might properly be, 'Anywhere', in the sense that God can take up any situation in our lives through which he communicates. But 'Anywhere' is too comprehensive and vague as an answer. Can we be more specific?

Let us not allow the qualifications in the answer to the previous question to dull our conviction that the Bible is a primary channel of God's word to us. By such means God confronts us with challenge, choice, guidance, rebuke and grace. A community of Christians that stops reading the Scriptures will soon be deaf to God and will make him after their own image.

In the sacraments, in preaching, in worship, Christians have affirmed God's presence and listened for his word. Not every sermon is an experience of encounter, but sometimes it happens! Again it has been part of the Church's experience that, when people are gathered for worship, they ought not to be surprised by God's coming.

However, we ought to note something important about the Bible's own witness. Many of the stories of God drawing near to his people are set in everyday contexts rather than specifically religious settings. The challenging word of God is heard through the prophet in the market-place or at the city gate. The injustices which humankind inflicts upon itself call forth from God a word of judgement and choice. Also, God's purpose is not only worked out through his own people (see Isaiah 45.1).

Could it be that through the politician's vision, the television documentary, the journalist's article, the novelist's story, the conversation at the bus-stop with a stranger, as much as at the prayer meeting, the communion service and the quiet moment of recollection, that we become aware of God and his lively word? If the answer to that is 'Yes', then we are faced with another important question.

How do we know it is God's word that we have heard? There are many who come claiming to speak for God. There are many who will quote the Bible passionately in support of their arguments for pacifism, against pacifism, for apartheid, against apartheid. How do we discern the word of God among all other human words?

'Knowing' in our contemporary minds often implies 'proving' and 'demonstrating', going beyond simply believing or expressing an opinion. Let us be quite honest and admit that if 'knowing' means being able to demonstrate and prove beyond logical doubt, then we do not know God and we cannot discern his word.

However, there are many things we claim to know although we cannot prove them. Scientific methods of knowing are appropriate for science but they do not fit, for example, with personal relationships. With these there is always the logical possibility of doubt, of being mistaken. No one can ever be in any relationship without risk, and yet it makes sense to talk of knowledge. We cannot prove beyond all doubt that someone loves us, but in the experience of life it makes every sense to say that we know we are loved.

So, how do we know it is God's word we have heard? Through generations the Church has worked at suggesting criteria which can be applied to any claim to have heard the word of God. For example:

(a) Scripture. Is what is said incompatible with the Jesus to whom the Bible bears witness? If someone claimed to have been told by God to destroy all black people, or Jews, or capitalists, then we would say they were mistaken. Their claim is incompatible with the Jesus of the Scriptures. So the Bible, with the Gospel pictures in particular, becomes an important criterion.

(b) The **tradition** of the Church. Christians believe that the Holy Spirit is given to keep and lead the Church in the truth. No one could claim that the Church has always been true to the Lord but, where there has been a consistency of teaching, in doctrine or morals, that has to be taken seriously. Contradicting the tradition would not automatically be wrong but an utterly new development needs to be wisely weighed against tradition.

(c) Reason. We spoke earlier about discerning the word of God. God has made us with minds to think and make judgements. The gift of human reason may not be highly prized in today's Church because in the past, perhaps, too much has been claimed for its powers. But it is hardly to be despised and neglected. Whether or not this is a word of God to us is something upon which we must decide. We must think about it.

(d) There may be **other criteria** to employ along with Scripture, tradition and reason. These may include our conscience, our intuitions, our feelings, especially when others we trust in the faith share the same perceptions and convictions. We believe that the Holy Spirit is continually opening our minds to new understandings of God's true word. However, feelings, institutions, appeals to conscience, and the Holy Spirit, only drive us back to the question: **How** do we know?

We have to recognise that faith is faith and not sight. Now we only see 'in a mirror dimly'. One day we shall know even as we ourselves are known by God (see 1 Corinthians 13.12). This does not mean that we cannot be addressed by God now and hear his word.

Our faith affirms we can. But what it also means is that there is a proper modesty in our claims that goes with receiving God's true word. There is a perfectly understandable longing in us for certainty. But we are human and not divine and, anyway, is it not possible that our lust for certainty is a reluctance to walk the more demanding path of faith? Those who ask for more than the insights of faith will always end up with less. Therefore . . .

How do we properly listen for God's word? This question requires a practical answer..

● First, there is the reading of the Bible, the record of the all-important self-revelation of God in Jesus.

● Secondly, by paying attention to the teaching of the Church in the past and in the form of what other Christians are saying today.

● Thirdly, by having faith in God, by praying – and thinking!

● Fourthly, by listening to other voices in our society, in the news, on television . . . , especially those that claim rights for others, or are struggling against injustice. Let us keep our ears open.

● Finally, by keeping our minds open. We have seen in our Bible readings in this chapter that sometimes God's people refused his word because they had decided beforehand what he was going to say. If what they heard was different from what they thought or believed it must have been wrong. That is the attitude of those with closed minds. It is not the attitude of faith. This is not to say that the new is always right, just as it is foolish to say that the traditional is never wrong. There is always before us the challenge of discernment. It is a call to our personal and corporate responsibility. At times we shall make the wrong choices. But we shall never be right at all if, when God comes to us with his word, we have already closed our minds and our hearts to his coming.

A prayer

God of all truth and goodness, you spoke in the great works of creation, in the challenge of the prophets, but above all in Christ Jesus. Still you long to communicate your word and will to us. We thank you for the Bible, for those who gave their lives that we can read it. We thank you for scholars, translators and interpreters, and all who help us in our understanding. May your word continue to inspire, rebuke, challenge and direct our lives each day. Give us open, receptive and thoughtful minds and help us in our daily task of discerning discipleship, through Jesus Christ our Lord, Amen.

+ Prayer of light
for forgiveness

Some questions and suggestions for further thought

1   What advice would you give to new Christians about ways of reading the Bible? If they asked you why they should read it, what answer would you give?

2   Can you think of any situations where you have been convinced about what God has wanted you to do? What features of these strike you as being particularly significant?

3   All of us have changed our minds over some issues of understanding the faith in the course of our Christian pilgrimage. What are the most important changes you have made?

4 There are organisations which send Bibles and other
   Christian literature to churches where such
   resources are very limited and rare. Could you
   arrange for your church to send some as a special
   gift this Christmas?

4
Prepare the way

At the centre of our readings in this chapter there stands the figure of John the Baptiser. He must have been a strange, unconventional and disturbing man. His message was one of urgency and challenge, and he spoke it without fear to high and low, to Jew and Gentile. In essence it was that God was about to do a new thing. The ancient words of promise were to be fulfilled and the rule of God would become present as never before. So John called for repentance. This was something more than feelings of sorrow and shame; it entailed a more active response, a turning around, a new way of living towards God.

This repentance was the necessary work of preparation for the new age. We, too, are into the business of preparation because Christmas is not many days away. But what does it mean to prepare for the coming of God? This is the question that takes us into the third week of Advent.

A word of strong comfort   Isaiah 40.1–11

These are the opening verses of the prophecy of Isaiah of the exile, the second Isaiah. Several prophetic books, like Jeremiah and Isaiah 1–39, begin with the record of the calling of God's messenger. This book begins, not with the messenger, but with the message.

Some Old Testament scholars suggest that we have to put the opening verses of this reading in the context of the heavenly court. Here is a picture of God taking council with those around his throne. It is given to a prophet to overhear what is being said. By this means he is able to speak to the people and tell them: 'Thus says the Lord.'

On this occasion God's word is one of comfort to his people. After the years of humiliation, which Israel had brought upon herself, God is to end his people's suffering and their days of slavery. The message is one of comfort and the call goes out for a way to be prepared for God. We almost get the sense that action must be taken quickly because he is already on his way, coming to save his people.

One feature of Babylonian life that the people of Israel in exile could hardly have missed was the New Year festival when the gods – idols – of Babylon were carried to the temples. There was a particular street down which the procession came, bearing the gods. Now Israel is called to prepare a way for God in the desert. In biblical imagery the desert or wilderness is often that area which stands between God's people and their home. Mountains must be lowered, valleys filled in, so that there is an uninterrupted way along which God can come. And as he returns to Jerusalem, in this very public act, so all the world will see who it is that reigns in history. God's glory will be revealed, and the prophet declares that God himself has promised this. Let the people be ready!

There is another voice which cries out, one that we cannot identify. It is called to affirm a vital difference between God and humankind. In the world of human affairs, change and decay are the normal state of things. Life is compared to grass – here today, but gone tomorrow. The life of the nation seems to be no more enduring than that. But God is different. The plight of the exiles may well appear to be helpless, but underneath all the changes and chances of life there abides the purposive love of God. In particular, God has already spoken his word of comfort, so comfort there will be.

So let the good news sound out! In Babylon and in Jerusalem let the people say that God is coming! In the return of Israel to Jerusalem the whole world will see who it is that really rules in history. The triumph will be very public.

In Isaiah 40.1–11 the prophet uses imagery similar to that of the exodus in order to speak of another great act by which God will set his people free. Together these two events declare God's faithfulness to his people in covenant love. They proclaim God's action for the oppressed and poor.

We mentioned earlier the way in which the gods of Babylon had to be transported to their temples. They had no power, no movement of their own; they had to be borne by humans. But Israel's God is not like that. He it is who carries his people, all of them together, and brings them home.

It is given to the prophet to speak a great word of hope to a dispirited people. It is not a word of faint optimism that all things will work out well in the end. Rather, it is a word about God, his nature and purpose. He is faithful to his covenant promise. He it is who is at work in history. He has taken the initiative that will bring about the people's liberation. God is coming to save – so make ready!

Who can survive God's coming? Malachi 3.1–5

Malachi is actually a Hebrew word meaning 'my messenger' – it is unlikely to have been a person's

name. These oracles that complete the Old Testament
come from a prophet about whom we know virtually
nothing. One consequence of this is that it is very
difficult to put the message of the book into its context,
but we can make an intelligent guess.

The prophet of the exile, the second Isaiah, had
brought a glorious word of hope and encouragement to
the Israelites. That word was fulfilled as, through
military and political changes, it became possible for
them to return home to Jerusalem. However, many
chose to remain in Babylon where their homes and
businesses were. They were not without God's
presence and, anyway, what was there for them back
home now? There was Jerusalem, of course; but the city
was in ruins. There was their own land; but the
territory was small and to make a living from it would
have been hard, and often unrewarding, work.

Some, nonetheless, did return. Doubtless they came
with high-hearted hopes and great ideals; but, frankly,
they were disappointed. Their dreams soon became
shattered on the hard rocks of reality. So we have a
situation of discouragement. With spirits falling
religious life came to a low ebb. The priests became
perfunctory in their work, and worship became more of
an offence to God than something well-pleasing to him.
Inevitably their moral vision dimmed as well. It seems
from Malachi that marriage, or rather increased
divorce, was a particular problem; but that was not the
only way in which society showed signs of breaking
down. All this led to questions, complaints and
challenges to God. It all seemed to come to focus in the
question borne of frustration and disappointment:
'Where is the God of justice?' (Malachi 2.17).

The sceptical spirit of the age had undermined faith in
the righteous God. What is the point of trying to live a

life that pleases God when all you get from it is struggle and poverty, while sinners bask in precisely those blessings which you hoped God would give you? The prophet's answer is in Malachi 3.1–5. A messenger will be sent by God to prepare the way for God's coming. Then the Lord, about whom the people are asking all those questions, will suddenly appear in his temple. First, there will be the messenger with the call to preparation; then, the coming of God.

But before Israel gets overexcited there is another question: 'Who can endure the day of his coming?' The messenger, bearing the word of God, will have an effect which they do not necessarily desire. Initially, there will be the testing and purifying of the priests and the whole of Israel's worship. Only in this way will what the people offer be pleasing to God. Verse 5 follows on this theme. There will be God's own testimony against all kinds of evil-doers – those who break God's commandments, those who cheat their workers, those who abuse the vulnerable and the stranger. Will any of these be able to endure the day of God's coming? Advent will indeed show that there is a God who is just, but who will be able to stand before him? Only those who presume upon God, or think more highly of themselves than they ought, can look forward with ease to the Advent of God. Perhaps, if the messenger were recognised and people responded to God's call, then at least they would be prepared for God's appearing. But if they did not listen, then what . . . ?

We need to note the following contrast, briefly mentioned in chapter 1 (pages 17–18). The foolish, immoral and unthinking in the Old Testament looked forward to the Day of the Lord with thoughts of blissful impunity. Those who were more perceptive were properly cautious. They heard the prophet's words about judgement and fire. Yet, in the New Testament, that day is looked forward to not in careless ignorance but in hope and longing for the coming of the Christlike God. We shall come back to this contrast again.

Divine and human judgement 1 Corinthians 4.1–5

Paul had a major part to play in establishing the Christian Church in Corinth but it cannot be said that his relationship with the congregation there was always easy. Sometimes people today suggest that we need to get back to the experience and practice of the early Church. But was Corinth that desirable?

Part of 1 Corinthians is Paul's reply to 'matters about which you wrote' (7.1), but the opening chapters are concerned with issues Paul wants to raise with the church in Corinth. He has heard some rather distressing and serious things about these Christians.

Certainly, they had squabbles about leadership. Paul, under God, had been the founder leader of that church. But there appears to have been those in Corinth who were not impressed by Paul's ministry. There were other leaders whom some members thought were more discerning, more knowledgeable and more spiritual than Paul. Corinth was a major seaport and, as such, was open to all kinds of influences and religions. Some of these religions had their own mysteries and secret knowledge into which the new adherents were initiated. It may be that some people with this background had become involved with the Christian congregation.

In Paul's view, people were adopting fundamentally wrong attitudes towards the leaders of the Church, comparing and contrasting them according to their own judgement. Paul does not become fearfully defensive. In his own heart he knows that he is called to be an apostle, called of Christ himself (1.1); but he also wants to say that all leaders are nothing in themselves. Indeed, they are particularly foolish if they think they are especially spiritual or wise.

Paul believes that the leaders should be looked upon for what they are – Christ's servants. He does not use the usual Greek work for slave or servant, but one that means 'secretary', 'minister' or 'assistant'. As such these leaders are in the employ of Christ. It is his purpose they are called to serve. They are not the personal possessions of some religious club which the members can simply discard in favour of the next year's model.

In particular, Paul asserts that the leaders have been put in charge of 'the mysteries of God' which are now revealed in the gospel. They are people who are entrusted with God's truths and it is to the Lord, not to the local fan club or critics, that they are to be faithful. This, for Paul at least, is the primary calling.

The consequence of all this is that the leaders must see themselves, and be seen, in this light. If the Corinthians expect their leaders to be something extra special, has Paul failed because he does not match up to their expectations? This does not matter – it is not their job specification he is called to fulfil. It may be that some leaders have stooped to curry favour in order to gain a reputation for themselves, but not Paul. He has refused to act in this way. His conscience is clear on that point.

The important perspective on all this is that it is the Lord who will pass judgement. How can we ever know the secrets and motives of one another's hearts, for we can only judge by outward and human standards?

Judging others in this way means that we often deal with them unfairly and cruelly. The thought of God coming to judge is, in fact, a liberating thought for Paul. Nothing will escape that divine judgement. Human praise and blame are really out of place in the Church. Paul will never engage in that; he will wait upon God's evaluation.

No gloomy season   Philippians 4.4 – 9

After some of the rather heavy themes of judgement and preparation we come now to a reading containing authentic New Testament high-hearted happiness. 'Rejoice in the Lord always; again I will say, Rejoice' (verse 4). Paul's letter to the church at Philippi constantly sounds this note.

The Advent theme is there in verse 5: 'The Lord is at hand' – he is coming soon! What does it mean to live believing this, holding the thought of God's coming before our minds? For Paul, the thought of the Lord's nearness changes so much for him. It is itself the ground of the Christian's rejoicing. His attitude is not one of casual flippancy, the easy-going happiness that rests on chance. It is based on the conviction that God is Christlike. Paul knows he is living on the resurrection side of the cross; it is the crucified and risen Lord who is near.

Living in this light does not mean that all life is now straightforward, uncomplicated, without anxiety or sorrow. Paul has more than enough to make him anxious and the Christians in the church at Philippi have also known threats and dangers. But Paul bids them to keep God at the forefront of their minds – God who is greater than all their troubles.

There is no denying the inevitable anxieties of life but these can be replaced with prayer and supplication. By praying faithfully we can hand over our anxiety to God. This is no stoicism, or joyless determination to see it through whatever happens. This is the life of faith in the Lord who is near, who creates the future, who has overcome and will overcome. So Paul can speak about God's peace, his gift of assurance, that guards our hearts and minds. Faith shows itself in asking for God's help and in prayers of thanksgiving. Thus it is that gentleness, joyfulness and kindliness are the marks of the Christian community. Christians are called to live like those servants who are expecting their master (see Luke 12.36).

The Advent imagery is sombre at times. The coming of God and judgement are not matters to take lightly. But Advent is not a gloomy season. It is a time to affirm hope – hope in God. And because he is coming, 'Rejoice . . . again I will say, Rejoice!'

The messenger's true importance   John 1.19 – 28

Some scholars of the Fourth Gospel suggest that, in some towns, alongside the growing Christian Church, there had continued groups of disciples of John the Baptiser. Certainly the author of the Gospel makes it obvious that he is putting John in his place! What is that place? The reading spells out the answer in two parts:

● First, the religious leaders ask who John is and he replies by saying that he is not the Christ – the Messiah (verse 20). This is hardly an answer to the question, but it does say something very important. John the Baptiser is **not** the Christ. Any who claim that in John can be found the message and way of God's salvation are deluded. Nor is John Elijah, or the special prophet who is expected to announce the coming of the Messiah. Who then is John? The answer is found in verse 23 in a quotation from Isaiah 40.3. The fact that John is ministering in the wilderness is seen as fulfilment of this word. He is the one who calls others to be ready for God's coming. That is what he is and that is all he is.

This is not to demean John. It is to give him his true worth and to indicate his importance. It is so easy for preachers and leaders to seek for themselves a glory greater than is theirs. Our natural self-seeking pushes us forward towards the light of recognition. We want that recognition, not least for the Church. But neither preacher nor Church is the gospel. We exist to point to the One who alone can lead us into liberty because he is the light. John is not all-important but he points to the One who is. John is a witness; he is not the Christ.

● Secondly, John's activity centres on helping people to prepare for the One who is to come. That is the meaning of the baptism to which he calls everyone. It is not by his baptising in water that John brings new life, only the Christ will do that. But there is a need to be prepared for One who is even now present but unrecognised (verse 26). John is not worthy even to untie Jesus' sandals – the task of a slave. By saying this John indicates the greatest possible distance between himself and the One whose presence he announces.

By the third week of Advent the people in many homes will be busy getting ready for Christmas. John the Baptiser had the task of getting the people of Israel ready for the coming of the Messiah. He called on people to repent, to change their ways. He was the announcer, not the programme. But what he said is of startling significance for us. Those who did not listen, who are not prepared, may miss the main event. This would be tragic, but so would be a response so impressed with the prophet that the message of God is hidden by the glory of man.

Do we look for another?   Matthew 11.2–15

It is tempting to speculate a little on what was going on in John the Baptist's mind when he was locked up in prison. In his ministry he had identified Jesus as 'he who is to come'. Had he been right in that?

There is no way in which we can get into the mind of John the Baptiser and identify his expectations and what raised the doubts in him. However, let us stay a little longer with the issue because it raises the important question of criteria. How would anyone discern the coming of God's Messiah and his saving presence in the world?

Jesus does not answer John's question in verse 3 with a straight 'Yes' or 'No'. Rather, he asks John's disciples to report back what they have seen and heard of his ministry. Miracles are happening, although Jesus himself does not claim to be a miracle-worker. What Jesus points to are the works of God, and he points to these not as proof of who he is but as signs for those who have eyes to see. Behind verse 5 there are echoes of Isaiah 35.5–6 and 61.1. Here are indicated the actions associated with the Old Testament hopes of the coming redeemer. Whatever John and his disciples may have had in mind these are the criteria of some of the prophets.

We ought to note especially that there is no mention in the Isaiah verses of cleansing lepers or raising the dead. They are added here presumably because they are part of the account of what Jesus has done. The claim is clearly that the coming of God's reign is not something that is about to happen; rather, in these events, it is already happening. Either these deeds are to be seen as the active presence of God or they are of no greater significance than the miracles which other people are performing. Those who do perceive the truth are blessed (verse 6).

This is what the reading affirms – in the life and deeds of Jesus, in the healings and in the proclaiming of the good news to the poor, God's kingdom is already present and active. Do we believe that Jesus is the coming One, or do we look for another? That is a question about our loyalty and our faith.

In the reading Jesus asks the crowd about John. How do they see him? What do they think of his ministry? Surely, when they went out into the wilderness they did not expect to see reeds shaking in the wind or a man dressed in soft, luxurious clothes. These things are not found in deserts. So what were the people looking for? A prophet perhaps? Yes, but there are two important things to say:

● One is that John is indeed a prophet, but of a special kind. He is the one called to prepare the way for God's coming salvation. As in John 1.19–28, this is the precise but important role John must play. He stands in continuity with the prophets but, in a crucial sense, completes their work. Why?

● Because – and this is the second thing – he stands on the brink of the new age. He does not himself belong to it but he is its herald. That is why, great as John undoubtedly is, the least in the kingdom is greater than he. People went out to see a prophet but they saw more than that. Until then, all the words God had spoken, through the law and the prophets, looked forward to the new age of God's saving purposes. Now John announces their coming. He announces the coming of the King and, as such, he stands on the edge of the kingdom. His question to Jesus is not just his own; it belongs with the whole challenge of John's ministry. Is Jesus the coming One – or do we still wait for another?

Here is one last thought about this reading. Thinking about reeds and soft clothes in the wilderness is dreamland. Perhaps it represents an idealistic view of God's coming with thoughts of luxurious living in a land of ease and plenty. But what is found in the desert is a man with a stern and uncompromising message, a challenge to repentance and heightened readiness for God. There is no talk of God's grandeur here, no easy promise of success, instant peace or unlimited plenty. So also the coming of God is to be found not in palaces and wealth but in a stable with the poor – and on the cross. Can this truly be the One? Or would we rather have another?

Some personal reflections

Out of a number of possible themes for reflection, here are four:

Isaiah 40.3 – 4 pictures the construction of a great highway running direct from Babylon to Jerusalem. There is to be no obstruction of any kind as the Lord leads his people home. Every mountain is to be levelled out and every valley filled in. So the Lord's way will be straight, direct and unencumbered. And with this comes the call of the prophet to prepare the way.

What might we think of today as obstacles standing in the way of the kingdom of God? What metaphorical mountains and valleys can we recognise that need the attention of those who seek to prepare for the Lord's coming?

Our personal and corporate pride must be dealt with. There are mountains of racial prejudice that some must try to clamber over before they can see the Lord's coming. Legislation can only partially deal with such racism. Fundamentally, hearts and wills need to be re-directed. This is not simply a comment on society. It is a word also addressed to the churches. Have we, by our attitudes, created some mountains that cannot be climbed? Why have we had the emergence of separate white and black churches? Is this the right way to prepare for the Lord?

In Europe we have built 'mountains' of butter, beef and other commodities. We have over-produced while, at the same time, in other parts of the world, thousands have died from starvation. There are all kinds of sophisticated reasons why this situation is not easily dealt with, but many of us feel offended by what has happened. The poor are not fed – yet enough food is produced for all. If we are going to prepare for God's coming then we must repent of political and economic systems that can lead to such injustice. Injustice, in any form, stands as a challenge to the rule of God. Wherever injustice, prejudice, unrighteousness and greed reign, there is the need for repentance. Preparing the way of the Lord entails political action.

And what valleys need lifting up? There are many kinds of hopelessness and despair in our world. Think of the young people in many parts of the world who already feel themselves diminished by the prospect of long-term unemployment; those who are moved about from country to country as refugees; and those who see their lives and dreams shattered by accidents or natural disasters. There are also those who live with deep depression, with AIDS or that fearful loneliness which exists in cities and villages alike. All these walk through valleys dark as death.

The Advent message is one of hope. Jesus' proclamation is that today God's promise of salvation is coming true. This takes some believing when we see unconquerable mountains before us or uncrossable valleys in our way. And it makes even less sense when the people of God are indifferent to these factors, as if they had no part in them and there was no need to prepare for the coming of God. There is a deep social challenge to be faced at Advent. John the Baptiser may have appeared as an odd and disturbing figure but his message rang true. In our modern wildernesses, we are called to prepare the Lord's way.

Malachi 3.1–5 makes us consider the relationship between worship and life, cult and ethics. The Lord who comes will purify both temple and society. It must be these two together because they are so intimately related.

Worship centres upon God. In an act of worship we try to bring our praise, prayer, offering, living, all before God and to God. Therefore, how we think of God in worship has massive consequences for the way we worship and the way we live.

Suppose that God had no real interest in the everyday life of this world – that he was untouched by human suffering and unmoved by human struggles, unconcerned with the kind of society that we create for ourselves – because his home was in heaven and what was fleshly and material was of no matter to him. To worship such a god would be to share his ignorance and indifference to the world.

Or, alternatively, suppose that the god we

worshipped was excessively nationalistic. He was **our** god, the god of **our** fathers. His promises were to us and, by definition, not to others. For them to be part of his blessing, they would have to become one of us. He would rule over all but only to punish others and save us, who are his people. The worship that followed would lead to exclusive rather than inclusive acts of worship and forms of community. Some would feel themselves shut out, separated, second-class, while the 'in crowd' would smugly rejoice and respond to others with demeaning indifference.

But, now, look at the God who has shown himself to be in Jesus, the friend of sinners, the one who loves Jews, Samaritans and Gentiles, who sends rain on the just and unjust. Moreover, this God and Father of Jesus Christ is One who, as Malachi implied in his prophecy, is at work in history despite all appearances to the contrary. If we know these things to be true, then there will be a properly inclusive, 'worldly' and social emphasis to our worship which will show itself in committed prayer and offering, with deep thankfulness for grace upon grace.

Malachi had strong words of judgement for the priests and worshippers of his day. They maintained the cult but their lives were far from God. That was apparent in the social injustices of the nation. A great gulf had opened up between ethics and worship. We might reflect on this for ourselves today.

The theme of judgement was prominent in 1 Corinthians 4.1–5. Paul speaks of God's judgement in positive and liberating terms. How can this be? There are two comments to make:

● First, Paul knows that it is before the judgement seat of Christ that we must all appear. We shall not be confronted by an unknown, arbitrary and temperamental judge, but by one who, in Jesus, has shown himself to be for us. This does not mean that we can take our sin lightly; nor does it mean that judgement is not truly awe-ful. Christ will be our judge, so we shall not be met by the coldness of law alone but by love – such love that 'while we were yet sinners Christ died for us' (Romans 5.8).

In one sense that makes the judgement even more awe-ful. Our offence is not simply against formal law and prohibition; it is against the Christlike God, it is the abuse of love. Yet this is the love that judges, that does not come to condemn but would purify and redeem us by suffering for us. This is divine love that will not let us go. No one can see this truth and be complacent about sin. Yet, paradoxically, the thought that Christ will be our judge is comforting.

● Secondly, Paul finds the thought of divine judgement liberating for this reason. We are all influenced by others and often look for the approval of those we admire. That influence can sometimes be very strong, so strong that our desire to please our heroes can become all-consuming. Our personal freedom is then given over to serve their ends.

None of us escapes judgement by others. Further, none of us escapes the kind of judgement, not always true and kind, which we make of each other in the Church. False witness is sometimes borne. Rumour can hurt and almost destroy us. This can produce a natural anxiety. We want to please. But then we can become so dominated by the desire to please others, that our consciences become compromised and our judgements become less than sincere.

By contrast, the thought that, in the end, we answer only to God is liberating. Our consciences need not be compromised. We can be true to ourselves before God. This may be painful. It also involves a massive responsibility to keep our consciences informed and our minds open to new truth. But to live to please others is a form of slavery. Paul knows that the people in Corinth compare him unfavourably with other leaders, but he resists the temptation to be like them. He will be true, as far as he knows his own heart, to God, the only judge that ultimately matters.

We can put it like this: when we stand before God our Judge, he will not ask us, 'Why were you not a Martin Luther, or a John Wesley, or a Billy Graham, or a Mother Teresa?' but he will ask, 'Why weren't you the person I called you to be? Why weren't you yourself?'

Lastly, we return to John the Baptiser. We have seen how the Gospels affirm that he has a very significant and important part to play in God's purposes; but it is clearly a very limited part. John must point to one who is greater than he. He must not seek any personal glory, no chosen followers. His is a supporting role in the divine drama.

It takes real grace to play that role. There is in all of us the desire to be noticed, praised, honoured and acknowledged. Ours is a competitive world, so it is not easy when the older person is bypassed for promotion by the young, able high-flyer. We may recognise the greater worth of that person but only the dishonest would not admit to just a little inward disappointment. John plays the supporting role that is his. He does not try to be the star, nor does he attempt to make himself indispensable. That takes grace.

One of the temptations before the Church is to make

a name for itself, to receive notice, praise, honour and status in the world. But the Church, the body of Christ, is called like the Lord to serve God's purposes. In Christian terms, the Church participates in and proclaims God's kingdom. It is not itself the kingdom.

Whenever the Church has believed that its own boundaries mark out the territory of the kingdom of God, then all kinds of bad consequences have followed. Not the least, the Church becomes blind to that activity of God beyond its own life.

Some of Israel's leaders had that problem. They had already determined the limits and form of God's rule. It did not include the child in the manger and the man on the cross. He was seen as a threat to their kingdom. They did not perceive, in consequence, the kingdom of God among them.

The Church participates in the purposes of God and has a crucial role to play in his kingdom's coming on earth; but it is not itself the goal. We can make an 'idol' of our church. If we do, then we have forgotten the role of John the Baptiser. We have confused the messenger with the message.

A prayer

Thank you, Lord, for all those who announce your coming in word and deed. You have called us to prepare your way. Make us bold to challenge all that dares to stand against your rule. Give us eyes to see your works of love and liberation today, that in quiet service we may again and again rejoice in your love. Amen.

Some questions and suggestions for further thought

1 In what ways do you understand John the Baptiser's preparatory work to be relevant to us today?

2 What mountains and valley obstacles do you think need removal before the Lord comes?

3 Preachers can often be discouraged. How do you think the Church might help them to be strong in faith? What encouragement have you given recently?

4 Life is very busy now, so near to Christmas. Plan how you can take 'time out' for yourself and your personal preparation to welcome Christ.

5
Annunciation!

It is only a few days to Christmas now. The readings for the fourth Sunday in Advent focus on the news that a baby is to be born. The fourth candle in the Advent wreath shines with the others in promise of the light of God even now coming into the world.

A particular theme to look out for in the Bible readings is that of change. People are called to a new obedience. Some individuals are challenged to respond in ways which mean that their lives will never be the same again. And, more than that, the whole of creation is affected by the coming of God's salvation. The scope of change is ultimately cosmic.

Anyone who goes through the Christmas season without being in some way changed by the message has probably not really heard that message of deep and radical challenge at all. How can any of us enter into God's salvation and remain exactly the same as before?

A new kind of king   Isaiah 11.1–9

This is one of the great and evocative prophetic readings of the Old Testament. For a long time it has been read in the Advent season and so has become associated with the coming of Christ. It is important, however, to put it into its own context. These verses are from the first Isaiah, a prophet in Jerusalem eight centuries before Christ. It is possible that he was himself related to the royal family. Certainly he lived and worked at a politically critical time for Judah. Earlier in the century the nation had enjoyed material prosperity but this was at the cost of much social injustice and corruption. Moreover, the nation was not so politically strong and independent as it had been and was now threatened by powers from the north. The leaders of Judah were quick to look for alliances with other nations. However, Isaiah saw the judgement of God coming upon a less than righteous people. He called them to put their trust in God again and seek his righteousness.

At the close of the previous chapter (Isaiah 10.28 – 34), the prophet pictures the enemy coming down from the north, taking the key-towns one by one before 'shaking his fists' at Jerusalem. But his word is that the Lord will deal with this enemy. He then uses the metaphor of trees in a great forest being brought crashing down as the axe is wielded against them. The overthrown enemy is pictured as a devastated forest.

Isaiah 11 begins with the image of a cut-down tree. But it is not dead, and a new branch will sprout from its stump. Even so shall a new king come from David's line. The prophet pictures this ideal king and the consequences of his reign. Significantly, the Spirit of the Lord will be upon him and by that Spirit he will have the necessary gifts to serve the nation under God. He will have intellectual and practical gifts – gifts of wisdom and skill to rule the people. He will be able to discern God's commands and will take pleasure in doing his will. Unlike other rulers in Israel the new king will not be swayed by human advisers with their self-interest to prompt them. He will defend the poor; he will judge fairly; he will care for the vulnerable; he will rule with justice and integrity. In other words, here will be the perfect king, perfect because he acts precisely in the way and will of the Lord. He will be a devout king, who knows the Lord, because God has given him his Spirit.

In the Bible, knowing God has intellectual, experiential and practical aspects. It involves mind, heart, strength and soul, and describes a whole way of life. Such a person is the king described by the prophet.

The consequence of this new king's reign will be a total transformation of all creation. The animals which now prey upon one another will live in peace. Even the lions will no longer shed blood to feed. And, most extraordinarily of all, a child and a snake will play together. All evil will be reversed. On Zion's hill, at the dwelling-place of God, there will be peace. And not only at Zion – Jerusalem – because the whole earth will be full of the knowledge of God. All creation will be transformed in the reign of this king.

Everything will come to exist in proper harmony. In days when we begin to perceive ourselves as threatened by ecological crisis this ideal picture remains even more powerfully evocative. Still, it seems, creation groans, waiting and hoping.

Silence! God is coming   Zechariah 2.10 – 13

It is not improbable that Zechariah's parents were exiles in Babylon. When the opportunity came, they took their child with them back to Jerusalem. Zechariah's work as a prophet is closely linked with Haggai and finds its focus in the rebuilding of the temple in Jerusalem around the year 520 BC.

It is not just the temple that is Zechariah's concern. He also calls the people to a new life and hope in the coming messianic age. His prophecies seem to originate in visions he is given. Our reading follows one such vision – a vision about measuring Jerusalem. The new Jerusalem is not to be measured according to its old design because that ancient fortress could never contain the many who will now seek to come to the dwelling place of God. The vision pictures a city without walls, with God in the midst, the glory of his people.

So, in verse 10, there is a call from God for the people to be alive in hope and joy. He is coming to live with them. We must remember that part of the anguish for the people of Israel during their exile years was the sense of God's absence. They were in a strange land. Where was God? They made the discovery that God was not confined to his holy place, the temple in Jerusalem, but could be with them even in their disgrace and humiliation. Now the prophet speaks again of God living with his people.

When the nations of the earth see this happening they, too, will acknowledge God and come to be his people. The nations, some of which have been the scourge of Israel and Judah, will themselves turn to God. That is one of the ways by which Israel will know God's presence as other nations too begin to make pilgrimage to Mount Zion.

Verse 12, with its reference to Judah being a special people, does not really conflict with the wider view of verse 11. The story of God's choice of this nation is the story also of her responsibility to reflect God's light to all the nations. Zechariah sees that happening. God will restore Judah and by that action the nations will see who really is God.

Verse 13 reads like a liturgical command, almost a call to worship. God is coming to be present with his people. Let there be silence! Let God's coming be greeted with awe!

Boast in the Lord!   1 Corinthians 1.26 – 31

One of the things about the church at Corinth which displeased Paul immensely was their party spirit. They were divided into cliques and inevitably began to be competitive, proud and uncharitable. In particular, they had problems concerning spiritual gifts. Some people were over-impressed by the more obviously exceptional and dramatic manifestations of the Spirit. Those who had received these gifts acted as if they were super-spiritual and definitely superior to the rest of the church members. They gave Paul a great deal of trouble, not least because they thought that they were in a higher class than Paul.

There were several consequences of all this boasting. The members split into groups and the church suffered the pain of divisions. Then, as a result of some claiming to be superior, others were made to feel inferior. Those who were not one of the 'spiritual ones', those who did not have one of the more dramatic and startling gifts of the Spirit could easily believe themselves to be second-class members in the church. The other consequence was that inevitably, because of pride and boasting, human leaders began to receive and look for glory. Praise and honour was being given to them and not to God. The whole Corinthian church was in danger of losing its way.

So, in his letter, Paul takes them back to first principles. He begins by reminding them of who they were when God called them to the life in Christ. Very few of them could claim to be notable, learned, significant or leading members of society. Later in the letter, Paul comments on some very unsavoury characters – adulterers, slanderers, thieves; and then, in a flashing phrase to remind the Corinthian church, he says, 'And such were some of you' (1 Corinthians 6.11). The fact is that when God was calling his Church into being he seems deliberately to have chosen people who were weak, simple and insignificant in the eyes of the world. It is often the despised and rejected, the discarded and denounced, whom God calls into his service.

If this is so, then there can be no grounds at all for boasting. It could hardly be because the Corinthians were the most prestigious that God chose them. These church members have nothing of themselves to boast about to one another, let alone before God. They have wrongly evaluated their gifts and themselves. Do they not realise that the gifts of the Holy Spirit are not their personal possession as some kind of prize or achievement, but simply represent God's gracious activity in and through them? They have nothing to boast about, but everything to be thankful for.

The fact is that all Christian existence and usefulness rests on God's gracious calling of us and not on our merit. It is God who has brought us into union with Christ, whom God made to be our wisdom. Some of the Corinthians boasted of their wisdom and intellect. In Judaism, wisdom was often personified as the mediator between God and humankind. Paul insists that it is Christ crucified who is the power and wisdom of God. Once again it is what the world thinks weak and foolish that God has used for his own purposes. It is by Christ that we are put right with God, called to belong to him, and are set free for new life.

If all this is true in the Corinthians' experience, then they must not glory in one another (see 1 Corinthians 3.21). If they must boast at all, let them boast of what the Lord has done for them and what he is doing through them.

Let us recall for a moment the great song of Mary, which we call the *Magnificat*. She praises God for the great thing he is doing through her and thanks him because he has remembered his lowly servant (Luke 1.48). Later generations may well call Mary blessed indeed. But she will not boast of her privilege, she will praise only the Lord.

The city of God   Revelation 21.1–7

Here is one of those marvellous visionary readings from the last book of the Bible. First, we shall look at its imagery, and then try to express its great message of hope.

It begins with a new heaven and a new earth. To long for a new earth makes sense to us, but why a new heaven? The answer is because heaven and earth go together. Before the completion of all God's purposes and God being 'everything to every one' (1 Corinthians 15.28) people may have thought of heaven as distant, unrelated and unreal. But in the new age the old has disappeared and even the sea is no more. The sea represents those moving unstable waters of chaos, always threatening to break out and overwhelm. But the waters, and the fears to which they give rise, are no more. In this vision all life is being transformed.

The holy city comes from God. It must come from God because it is beyond humankind to build and design. It is the goal of a long quest (Hebrews 11.10), but it comes only as a gift. It is not just another city but a renewed city, belonging with the new covenant and the new life of resurrection. Just as the body is raised and transformed in resurrection, so is all creation raised and transformed in the new heaven and earth.

This holy city is new Jerusalem. We have already read

85

how some of the prophets in the period following the exile look towards the re-establishing of Jerusalem. A transformation beyond any nationalism is envisaged. Here Jerusalem represents a new social order.

The great pronouncement is that God's home is now with humankind. The Greek word used here means 'tabernacle', and a form of the same word is used in John 1.14 which speaks of the Word becoming flesh and dwelling with us. That 'tabernacling' in one human being is now being completed. There is no separated sphere or area for God, no temple in this new Jerusalem, because God is the light and life present in all in the city (see Revelation 21.22 – 22.5). God is with his people – God with us, Emmanuel indeed.

All the former things of heaven and earth, including sin and death, grief and pain, are no more. God heals and comforts, and tears are wiped away for ever. Such things belong to a form of life that has disappeared.

Then God speaks. In this direct form we know that any gaping gulf between God and humankind has been done away with. All things are made new. The present tense is used because the future promise is now fulfilled. The old evils are defeated. 'It is done' (verse 6) indicates completion. It reminds us of Jesus' cry of victory from the cross – 'It is finished' (John 19.30) – as he completed the work that the Father had given him to do and set the new creation on its way.

So God, the Alpha and the Omega, the first and the last, the beginning and the end, gives the water of life to the thirsty – that is, to those who know their need. The gift is grace, without price, and is summarised in a great relationship, 'I will be his God and he shall be my son' (verse 7). Nowhere in Revelation is God called Father – in this book the Father-son relationship is kept to denote the relationship between Jesus and the

Father. Now, in and through Christ, this is shared by all.

John's vision affirms that what had been established and set in motion by the resurrection of Jesus has now come to completion. This 'end' is anticipated and celebrated by Christians in their worship, especially in Holy Communion. This is a foretaste, for what is done at the table does not happen in the absence of God. Even so, the presence of God with us is veiled, but the faith and action point forward to what is to come. The Church which John knew had its own experiences of suffering, death and mourning. Living 'between the times' was not without tears. But, in faith, the faith was proclaimed – 'Behold, I make all things new' (verse 5).

These verses remind me of two pictures. In the vestibule of Bloomsbury Central Baptist Church, London, there is a painting depicting the many-sided life of the city of London. There is also the cross with the most needy people of all closest to it. The whole theme of the work is expressed in the proclamation included in the painting, 'Behold, the dwelling of God is with men.' It is a noble affirmation in central London of faith in the Christlike God. The other picture is a mural tapestry hanging in the chapel of the Northern Baptist College, Manchester. It shows the city of Manchester – the banks and business institutions, the town hall, the cathedral, the university, the hospitals, schools, shops and homes. The artist has gently shot the work through with gold and silver threads so that, as the light is shone upon it, this all-too-human city is transformed. When we gather for worship this vision of two cities is before us. When all things are made new, London and Manchester will be no more, but will be part of the new creation. Even so, in these cities now, God comes and makes his presence known.

Announcing a very special child   Luke 1.26 – 38

This is definitely a **Christmas** reading in the minds of many Christians, but let us try to stay with the theme of Advent. It is the story of annunciation, full of fascinating features that are so arresting that they tempt us to miss the wood for the trees.

In the Bible, the story-form of annunciation is well-known. Annunciation stories are told of Isaac, Samson, Samuel and, of course, John the Baptiser. To speak of them as stories is not to imply that they are all fiction. It is significant that they have a similar form. It is a form used when the writer or evangelist wants to make the readers aware of the special purpose which the one about to be born has in God's history of salvation.

However, this story proclaiming the coming birth of Jesus is not exactly similar to the others. There are significant differences that give us clues into the meaning of it all. Usually annunciation stories include a miracle that is surprising in the sense that it is out of the ordinary run of things but not impossible. So Isaac was born of elderly and supposedly barren parents. Hannah, too, had waited many painful years before the birth of Samuel. In Jesus' case the annunciation is to Mary, a young woman who is not yet married. In telling this story, the writer of Luke's Gospel lays emphasis upon the activity of the Holy Spirit (verse 35). The reason why this child is to come into the world is a much more significant matter than any argument about a biological miracle. Jesus is to be born, a human into human history, but he does not entirely come from the limited world of human affairs. The stress is on the divine origin of Mary's child.

It is in the light of this that we should try to understand the references to Gabriel and to Mary's virginity. To dismiss the whole as fantasy, or to insist that it is all historical fact, is to run the risk of missing the gospel proclamation that Jesus' Advent is the work of God. The story of Gabriel and the virgin birth indicates to the reader the specialness and the unusualness of it all. This child's coming cannot be told of or explained in only human terms.

Within the reading there is a great deal about the character of the child who is to be born. Some of the Old Testament is echoed in verses 32 – 33 which speak of the enthronement of the king. The language is Davidic, and any first-century Jew would know that you could hardly speak more highly of anyone than that. Although the mother is virtually unknown and her home town a place of no great consequence, this birth will be of the 'Son of the Most High' God, of a King. From such obscure surroundings is coming an event of the deepest religious and political significance.

In the story Mary makes three responses. First, she is troubled and afraid (verses 29 – 30). She does not know what the message means. It is beyond her comprehension. Secondly, as she hears that her cosy, familiar, small world is going to be opened up in the greater context of God's purpose she becomes perplexed (verse 34). Who wouldn't be? Then Mary accepts, saying, 'I am the handmaid of the Lord; let it be to me according to your word' (verse 38). In this, she acknowledges her identity before God. She takes up the part she must play in the divine purpose. Something new is about to happen. Mary does not understand, she is even afraid; but she is to be honoured because she submits herself to God's purpose and trusts herself to God's disturbing, surprising will.

The fulfilment of this annunciation – the coming of

the Son of God – cannot be without Mary's 'Yes' to God. There are certain things that are only possible with God, but let us not overlook the fact that God's Advent(ure) also involves a human readiness and acceptance. Advent is a divine initiative **and** a human response. A young woman's 'Yes' to God is a crucial part in God's new way of being present in the world.

Names and their meaning   Matthew 1.18 – 23

Here is the annunciation again but told in a very different way. In this reading, the angel comes to Joseph and it is Joseph's active response that is underlined.

Matthew's Gospel opens with sixteen verses of Joseph's family tree. The genealogy is set out in three groupings – from Abraham to David, from David to the exile, and from the exile to Joseph. Whoever comes next is heir to the whole history of God's chosen people, but he also comes from an unambiguously human line.

So the writer of Matthew sets out to tell of the 'birth' of Jesus. In the original Greek, the word used is *genesis*. It is *genesis* by the Holy Spirit. Is the Gospel writer making the point in his choice of words that a new beginning is being made, a new creation coming to birth?

Mary and Joseph were betrothed. This was absolutely binding, unlike 'being engaged' today. In our world 'being engaged' is a preliminary to enacting the marriage legally, but in the Judea of Jesus' time betrothal was the actual contract of marriage. This meant, for example, that if either partner had sexual intercourse with a third party, it was adultery. If the man died, then the woman was regarded as a widow. However, it was possible for the betrothed man to declare the woman's vows to be null and void, and 'divorce' her. Usually the betrothal lasted for one year. During this time sexual relations between the couple were not permitted. But while Joseph and Mary were betrothed, Mary found that she was pregnant.

In Matthew we read that Joseph was a just man – he wanted to do what was right. There is no way, of course, by which we can get into the mind of Joseph and be privy to all his many thoughts. He decides to resolve the situation quietly, with as little shame as possible. Then he has a dream in which an angel comes to him. The important thing for Joseph – and for us – is the message. Mary has conceived by the Holy Spirit. In law, the child's parents will be Mary and Joseph. But the coming of this child, of David's line, is not the result of human procreation – it is the work of God. That is what the writers of both Matthew and Luke want to proclaim.

So Joseph is told not to be afraid to take Mary as his wife. She will have a son and already the name has been chosen. In the Bible, names are important; they reveal something of the character and purpose of the person. This child is to be called 'Jesus' – the Greek form of the Hebrew name Joshua – which means 'Jehovah is salvation'. Jesus will save his people from their sins (verse 21). The important message of the angel amounts to an announcement of God's active involvement in history, his Advent in Jesus, the coming of God's salvation.

An important feature of Matthew's Gospel is the many quotations from the Old Testament. This is the evangelist's way of saying that all that is taking place is in the declared purposes of God. So, here in verse 23, he quotes from Isaiah 7.14. In their original setting these were words of hope and encouragement to Israel to keep faith with God. The political situation may look desperate and uncertain but a sign of God's continual blessing will be a woman bearing a child. Trouble may come, trouble that the people have brought upon their own heads but God is faithful. In the birth of the boy, God's presence will be affirmed. His name is *Emmanuel* – God with us.

In Luke's annunciation story we read of Mary, frightened and perplexed, accepting her part in God's purpose. Here, in Matthew, Joseph, once he has woken, shows his faith as he does what God's messenger has told him to do. He and Mary marry; and they call their son, born like any other son, Jesus.

Personal reflections

The season of Advent has its own impetus. Steadily we move towards a climax and the shorter the journey grows the greater the speed. The Gospel readings in this chapter show how near we are. The baby is conceived. Already he is growing in his mother's womb. It cannot be long now. Each day the moment comes nearer when anticipation will give way to event.

Anticipating has a vitality of its own. Hopes approaching fulfilment are hopes bursting with excitement. If you have a small child in your home as Christmas approaches you will be able to see and hear the excitement rising.

All biblical faith is anticipatory. The Old Testament looks forward as prophets and priests dream marvellous dreams of all things being renewed. And the New Testament does not lose that sense for, even though Christ has indeed come, faith in God shows itself in hope and anticipation of what is yet to be. To have faith in God is to look forward. It is never a matter of resting content in the present as if it were everything. However good today is, our salvation is coming with tomorrow, for it is out of the future that God comes to us.

This sense of faith as anticipation has been a feature of the readings for this week. There are, however, three issues that require our attention and reflection and all of them are a little bit thorny.

First, let us look at the matter of Mary giving birth to Jesus although she is a virgin. For many Christians this is a fundamental article of faith, expressed in the Bible and taught by the Church, and on that basis it is believed. But every Christian recognises the strangeness and the uniqueness of the affirmation. It does not fit in easily with our understanding of the rest of our experience.

It has been argued that what Matthew and Luke stress, more than any other consideration, is the activity of God in the coming of Jesus. There is no doubt that Jesus was a real flesh-and-blood child born, as Paul says, of a woman (Galatians 4.4). In this way Jesus belongs with our humanity. He shares it, in joy and pain. So he knew what it was to be hungry, to be a refugee in flight from a despotic ruler. He wept when bereaved. He bled when they stabbed him. He died, as we all shall, when the human body can take no more.

So Jesus is human. But it is not enough to say that he can be accounted for solely in terms of our humanity. The first Christians, mostly monotheistic Jews, found that they could no longer think of God without thinking of Jesus, not in spite of his humanity but because of it. God entered into human life and history in this man as never before. He belongs with David's line but his origin is not with the sons of David.

This is beginning to sound as though God took some special initiative here – did he intervene in the normal course of events for his own purposes? But there is a difference between initiative and intervention. People make interventions when they stand outside a situation. They come into that situation and get involved in what otherwise would simply happen without them. It is strange to think of God outside the life of the world and intervening only occasionally. That would make God only an occasional visitor and his activity a matter of fits and starts. However, if we think of God constantly at his work of creating and sustaining his creation, so that he is never outside and always working (John 5.17), this does not rule out the possibility of him taking special initiative. Those who rule out the whole possibility of God acting in the world, who deny all possibility of miracles, will not make any sense of this. But the Christian faith involves God's action. It is not always easy, however, to think of appropriate and coherent ways of talking about divine activity.

So, what of the virgin birth? If you believe the things that the Bible says literally just because they are in the Bible, then there really is not a question here for you. On the matter of virgin birth as a biological miracle, is it possible to be otherwise than agnostic? We just do not have the means necessary to settle the question. More than that, issues of translation of the Bible text and other matters of doctrine call the affirmation as a biological fact into question. But, in any case, this kind of questioning may lead us to miss the point in the Gospel writers' proclamation – the proclamation that, uniquely, God is involved in the coming of this baby as the focal part of his whole purpose of saving a lost humanity. Jesus is man for us **and** God for us; and 'in Christ God was reconciling the world to himself' (2 Corinthians 5.19).

This relation between the humanity and divinity of Christ leads us into the second matter for reflection. It causes us to think some more about one of the ways by which God actively works out his purposes in history.

The two Gospel readings in this chapter concern the response of Mary and Joseph to the initiative of God. We noticed how both of them accepted the different roles they had to play for the coming of Jesus as God's salvation. In 1 Corinthians 1.26 – 31, Paul argues that God does not necessarily call the great and good into his tasks, sometimes it is the seemingly weak and foolish in the eyes of the world through whom God acts. There are even incidents in the Bible of God acting out his purposes through those who do not acknowledge him. Cyrus of Persia is one who comes to mind.

Also, consider the calling of Moses in Exodus 3 where God says that he has heard the call of the oppressed and suffering people and that he will come to deliver them. Moses will share that work because he, too, has seen the injustice of the Egyptian slave-masters (Exodus 2.11–12). He has heard the cry that God has heard. Although he cannot be the liberator of Israel, he will throw his energies and life into sharing God's hopes and will. So it is that God liberates Israel from the land of slavery, but not without Moses. Similarly, Jesus cannot come without the 'Yes' of Mary.

God is God and not human; yet his coming is not apart from our humanity. In Jesus we see divinity in humanity and humanity in divinity. What has come to perfection in Jesus is what God is seeking in and through all humankind. He, who came to us and became incarnate in Jesus, is always seeking to incarnate his love in human life to the fulfilment of his purposes.

Now, finally a reflection on the nature of those purposes, with Isaiah 11.1–9 especially in mind. In a wonderful way the prophet spoke of the transformation of all creation, of all things being made new.

Today we are having to take greater thought for the future of our planet as we realise the extent to which we have already spread pollution. Greenhouses were once places where we nurtured and developed new plants; now the phrase 'greenhouse effect' has frightening and fearsome overtones.

Isaiah saw connections which we do not always make. He saw that there was a relationship between how we worship and what we do. If there is no connection between our acts of worship in church and the way we live in the rest of our lives, then we have opened up a dangerous gap. The prophet also saw a connection between God's hopes for humanity and his care for nature – between salvation and ecology. God seeks not only 'peace on earth and goodwill among men' but peace between people and the rest of nature. God's purposes and his coming salvation are pictured in cosmic terms. The coming of God will mean that nothing is left just as it is; all will be brought to a greater harmony, a deeper *shalom*. 'Behold, I make all things new,' says the God who came in Jesus and is still coming for the salvation of the world.

A prayer

Loving God, in your coming you make yourself vulnerable to our response. As we hear the announcement of your Advent among us, grant us grace to welcome you, to honour you, and to offer our lives in your service, that your love may take the form in us that you desire, through Jesus Christ our Lord, Amen.

Some questions and suggestions for further thought

1 What reflections do you have on what is said here about the virgin birth? How significant a doctrine do you think it is?

2 God is always seeking to incarnate his love in human life. Where in your own personal and corporate experience is there special need for that love to be present?

3 Look again at Isaiah 11.1–9. All creation is renewed. How do you understand this challenge of Advent?

4 Think of people who will be on their own this Christmas. Can you invite one or two of them to share the celebration with you? Who else might you especially remember at this time?

6
The good news of Advent

Each week in Advent, as we have read the Bible readings, we have been faced with a tension so persistent and prevalent that it must be essential to the faith. It is the tension between the present and the future. It shows itself in several ways.

For example, we have found ourselves affirming both that Christ is present with us and that he is still to come. In a similar way, we speak of the kingdom of God, present but still prayed for. We believe we are saved and yet we await our salvation. We are raised to life in Christ and yet look for the resurrection. The new age has dawned and yet is still to come.

If we lose this tension then something essential has gone from our faith. For example, if we say that everything is already achieved, then the harsh reality of life will bring us to the conclusion that God's salvation does not amount to very much. So much of our present life is obviously unredeemed. On the other hand, if we throw all our understanding of God's salvation into the future, then our faith is reduced to 'pie in the sky when we die'. Is there no good news of God's gracious work in the present?

Authentic Christianity knows the tension of **now** and **not yet**. We can celebrate and affirm our salvation and the presence of the kingdom, but not yet. Both present and future feature in the faith we proclaim and both relate to the past in which God has already acted in his liberating grace. If we believe in God's goodness today and look for the completion of all things as his salvation comes in the future, then it is because of what he has been and done in the past. Memory, presence and hope all belong together in the Christian faith. In this final chapter we shall reflect a little more on the main Advent themes in the light of this inherent tension.

The importance of hope

Hope is at the heart of Advent. It belongs in the very centre of Christian belief and life. We gain our Christian self-understanding not simply on the basis of our history but because of God's future. We are called to participate in that future. We have hope.

Some of the readings we have looked at come out of times of genuine despair. Our humanity is very frail and our best-laid plans and highest ambitions can quickly come down to the dust. We dream our dreams, construct our ideal utopias mentally, but the reality of life is something else. In honesty we recognise that it is not just others who are the problem. We fail to match our own expectations. We have our hopes, but they are beyond us.

Yet, so the Bible affirms, situations of human hope-lessness are not beyond the power of God to redeem. This is not to say that God simply takes up our hopes and fulfil our desires – in fact, these are often part of the problem because they can be so selfish and partial. Rather, it is the conviction that God can and will bring his purposes to completion. We have hope in the most desperate of situations because we believe in **God**. This God is the God of Abraham, Isaac and Jacob, the God of David and the prophets, of the exile and the return. Above all, this is the God and Father of our Lord Jesus

Christ, who in his Son knew the agony and horror of utter forsakenness even to death but who brought forth, even from the grave, the promise of hope and life. To believe in the God known in Christ is to believe the Advent hope, whatever life may bring. He is the God who is making all things new.

Therefore, to live the life of faith in the Advent hope is to share the purposes of God now. It is now that he is making new. Faith in God shows itself in setting out towards the future, in obedience and in trust that it is in the future that the God, who calls us in the present, will be met. Advent faith is not staying at home, waiting and hoping for something or someone to turn up out of the blue. It is to be like Abraham, to dream a dream, to get up and go, only then to discover the presence of the coming God (see Genesis 12.1–9).

Because God is the One who calls us into a future, which is his gift, it is our hope in that future which is the basis of our present confidence. So the Christian persists, in situations of costly discipleship and of demanding sacrifice, in hope of God. One of the things that the future hope is about is how we face the crises of life now. Of course, if we are in a desperate plight, beyond all our own resources, we may declare the situation hopeless and try to do nothing but endure. But, if God is Christlike, then we can believe that there is nothing in life or death to separate us from that divine loving purpose and, in consequence, we shall dare to do things as disciples because we have hope.

There is a tension between the future and the present to be kept here. It seems that in the early Church there were those, so obsessed by the thought of Christ's coming, that they abandoned all their present responsibilities, such as doing any work (see 2 Thessalonians 3.11). Hope without bearing the present responsibilities of our calling is not Christian hope at all. Christian hope in the coming of God shows itself in active obedience to God whose presence we know in his call upon our lives.

Such faith shows itself in many ways, not least in response to tragedies such as bereavement. A person's death reveals the limit of all human existence. The Christian, however, believes that not even death – whether because of old age, illness or accident – has the last and final word. That word is spoken by God, who spoke the first word in the beginning and who spoke in Jesus risen from the dead. At the end he will speak the word that finally counts. So even in death, with all its proper grieving, Christians are not without hope. We show that hope, not in any unrealistic, spurious triumphing that denies the reality of death and pain, but in that quiet trust that leaves the one we love with God and then continues in the present calling and responsibilities which God offers to us.

There is an incident in the life of Jeremiah that bears reflection here. The prophet's message was one of judgement and darkness – the people would experience the devastation of Jerusalem, exile and the loss of liberty. All their hopes as a nation were being severely called into question before God. But it was in this situation that Jeremiah bought a field (see Jeremiah 32). This was not the act of a land-speculator. Rather, it was an act of trust in God, expressing faith in God's future. It was a sign of hope.

To sum up, the Advent hope is one of hope in God. It is hope in God's coming to redeem and save us. In the face of our sin and death we have no hope but in God. Yet we believe in that coming God who is even now doing a new thing, working in the present to bring the future to birth. This is a costly, suffering work for

God, bearing our rejection and disobedience. The cross proclaims the creative suffering of the God whose will is to bring salvation to completion. To have hope, therefore, is to throw in our lot with the struggle of God today, to join the great adventure, to love and care whatever the cost and however dark the situation looks. To hope in God is to follow Christ today.

The importance of eschatology

Eschatology is that part of the faith concerned with the 'last things' – judgement, hope, the coming of God, the resurrection, the life eternal. All of these themes, consistently present in the ancient creeds, are part of the Advent message. Advent is the beginning of the Christian year, but we deal with the 'last things' first.

These great themes have one thing in common – they are all ultimate. When we come to the end all provisional judgements will give way before a final judgement, the ultimate word. The Christian faith takes history seriously because it is in history that we believe God has been at work in self-revelation, judgement and salvation. But history is to be completed. Whatever has appeared in human history is provisional, partial, penultimate. The eschatological themes of Advent affirm the finality of the work and purposes of God.

This is to affirm one part of the tension indicated in the introduction to this chapter. If we concentrate everything in the here and now and make its claims and perceptions absolute, then we lose the important Advent emphasis on the end. We shall consider how this can happen and see how dangerous the effect of misunderstanding the faith can be.

Christians believe that God has saved 'once for all' in

Jesus Christ. What is necessary for the world's salvation has been done. Christ's work, as earlier theologians used to say, is a 'finished' work. This is so, in spite of the fact that Paul recognises that there is more for Christ to do until all the kingdoms of this earth are gathered up in offering to God (see 1 Corinthians 15.24 – 28).

The tension that must be held is between the 'finished' work of Christ and the fact that clearly the kingdoms of this world do not belong completely and utterly to Christ. If the world we live in is saved, then it is obviously a limited salvation. An old story told among the Jewish rabbis makes the point. A foolish man got up on a mountain and blew the ram's horn, the sign that God's redemption was dawning. This act was reported to an old wise rabbi who opened his window, looked out on the world and simply said, 'This is no renewal.'

We Christians can take the point. In Christ, God has done that necessary work of our redemption but the world still awaits its fulfilment. If we do not hold this tension we may fall into the trap of identifying our present state as Christians with 'being saved'.

The danger is most obviously apparent when being a saved Christian is identified with participating in a particular culture or way of life. We give to our society – say English middle-class church-going respectability, or the great American dream, or a left-wing utopian vision – the status of living in the kingdom. The point is that, however good and worthy these social forms and ideas may be, they are all, at best, penultimate. They are not the fullness of salvation which God wills to bring. To suggest that they are everything would be to mislead and even blind people to a greater hope and glory. The content of the faith which concerns the 'last things' helps us rejoice in what God has given but saves us from making it everything because only God brings the completion when he will be all in all. A self-satisfied Christian is indeed one in desperate need of salvation.

Let us look at another illustration of the way in which the themes of the 'last things' bear important witness to the faith. This is an historical illustration, of a social and political nature, but it underlies how the Advent message affirms our true liberty. Adolf Hitler came to power in Germany at a time when the nation was still smarting and suffering the humiliation of the defeat of the First World War. Hitler appeared as a strong leader who helped the German people to recover pride but, as all the world now knows, his style of leadership became grotesque and authoritarian. He came to brook no opposition, no questioning of his policies. In other words, he made his nationalistic ideas and commands absolute. Many people became victims of this new form of slavery. Many, but not all. There were some who resisted these absolute claims and quite a number did so in the name of Christ. True, there were some Christians who, having lost the tension mentioned earlier in this chapter, saw Hitler as part of God's saving purposes. But there were others, like Karl Barth, Dietrich Bonhoeffer, Rudolph Bultmann, Martin Niemoller, who lived out the biblical faith and affirmed that in social and political terms only God in Christ could have the last and final word. They challenged the authorities of the day in the name of Jesus Christ the Lord. One of the forms by which God's liberating work took flesh was in the lives of those Christians who stood against evil and refused to acknowledge that it had absolute power.

That Christ alone has the last and final word is

liberating. It leads to the recognition that all human claims to our loyalty are relative, provisional and penultimate at best. To obey the words of people such as Hitler without question is to enter into slavery. But to give oneself to the absolute claim of God is to enter into that service in which alone true freedom is found.

This point applies not just to historical situations but to present-day concerns. Any politicians or leaders who lay an absolute claim upon us, or who insist that their policies alone are right, need to be challenged in the name of God. The Advent message entails, therefore, that there will be times when we shall be called upon to take sides. Advent expresses the faith that only what God wills is ultimately important and no human social system can claim to express absolutely the will of God. So, for example, to live the Advent faith would be to challenge apartheid, to take sides against those who insisted that their policy was unambiguously right. All our humanity in history has a provisional quality about it. We see only through a glass darkly. Modesty and humility characterise those who live the Advent faith.

The issue of judgement

Judgement figures strongly in the Advent readings. Sometimes, it expresses the point made above, namely, that the final judgement is with God alone. Whatever we think of ourselves, whatever others think of us, that is not the last word. The final judgement, the one that matters, is with God.

We have seen how this doctrine gives a great moral seriousness to life. We cannot sin with impunity as if our failure to be God's people did not really matter. One of the genuinely serious things about much of our contemporary world is how easily the notion of sin and judgement is made into a joke. We think that because we have become easy-going and undemanding with ourselves and one another that this tolerance of injustice and sin will be God's response also. But Advent warns us that it is not so.

As joking is not the way to face the theme of divine judgement, so the other extreme is equally unhelpful – that is when God the Judge becomes the ultimate and dominant image of God. I once met a person whose life had been dominated by the thought of God seeing, knowing, recording everything as if he were some great cosmic policeman. This man had no privacy and, therefore, had lost his individuality. He came both to hate and fear this insufferable judge. As a result of this picture of God – the image of unrelieved judgement – he lost all sense of self-worth and respect. He lived only to fail and feel guilty. God was in no sense 'good news'.

Neither of the above responses to God our Judge is Christian. One does not take judgement seriously enough, while the other views it too seriously. So what are we to say? Is there any sense at all in which the credal statement, 'I believe that he will come again to be our Judge', is good news?

We have already seen that to live in the conviction that God is our ultimate Judge is liberating because that immediately makes all human judgement relative. We are free from the anxiety of always having to please others by conforming to their expectations. In the service of God freedom is found. But all that belongs to the thought of God's final judgement beyond history. What about the theme of God's judgement now? Simply a glance at the Bible will affirm the faith that, even in the events of the world's history, God is working out his purposes of judgement and salvation.

God's present judgement in history can be understood in two ways. The first is to think of the whole cosmos being shaped by fundamental moral laws – 'laws which never shall be broken'. To offend against these laws means bringing a punishment upon ourselves, our children, or our children's children. This is a very impersonal kind of justice but we can see the point of it. For example, if we abuse our body we shall suffer physically. If we continue to pollute the atmosphere, then our children and grandchildren will have to pay a heavy price because of our poor stewardship – our imagining that we own the earth whereas we are only its custodians.

On the other hand, the Bible has more direct ways of affirming this aspect of God's work in history. One of the other tensions the Bible asks us to hold in our minds is that between the thought of God as our sovereign and of ourselves as mortal beings with the opportunity to exercise our free will. We can deliberately offend against God's laws, and thus be said to bring judgement automatically upon ourselves. However, we find Paul writing about God giving people up to the consequences of their actions (for example, see Romans 1.18 – 32). God actively and deliberately allows this judgement to happen, with all the consequences that follow.

So, in history, we are not simply dealing with a natural cause-and-effect relationship, but with the activity of God in judgement. We ought not to think of God as standing apart and aloof from all this, unresponsive and uncaring as if he were a cold judge handing down punishment. We have already seen how the Bible can think of God sharing his people's humiliation and failure. God knows the pain of our sinfulness. He, too, suffers in Christ the consequence of our sin.

This is not to say that God sends war as a judgement or AIDS as a punishment. We cannot be that glib, not least because we recognise that some who suffer in all this are innocent of the causes. To say that those children, presently being born with AIDS, are thereby being judged and punished by God is to make him an ogre.

If we allow this way of speaking about God, then we are bound to ask, 'Why doesn't God step in and punish the guilty and protect the innocent?' This is the old problem of evil which seems to imply either that God cannot, in which case he is not all-powerful, or that he will not, in which case he is not all-good. What is of vital importance at all times in this argument is that we keep as close to God's self-revelation in Jesus as possible. This finds its focus not in naked power but in the suffering love of the cross for and with us sinners. If we think of God in these terms then we see new dimensions to the love of the God who gives us over to our sin. However, far from stepping into the situation, he bears it with us because he is already in the situation.

This implies that the proper response to such judgement is not self-defensive excuses but honest confession and true repentance. Why doesn't God just scrap the whole mess we have made of the world? We cannot say. But we can believe that the Christlike God bears with us, suffering our shame and sin, while he struggles continually to bring from our disasters the new beginnings and further possibilities. He does not come to condemn, but comes to judge as part of his healing, saving purposes. So he calls us to repentance, to turn and walk in his ways.

The writer of the Fourth Gospel gives us one of the most powerful images of all. He speaks of Jesus as the light of the world. He also observes, rightly, that we seem to love darkness rather than light because our deeds are evil. Jesus comes as the light of the world to reveal the way, the truth and the life for us. He does not come to condemn. But an inevitable effect of his coming is to show the darkness up for what it is. So the Son of God, our Saviour, is our Judge. The question is: Will we, or will we not, live in the light? God has given us challenge and choice. 'Now,' said Jesus, 'is the judgement of this world' (John 12.31), because even now the light of Christ shines, for healing and for judgement.

Until he comes

We have made a journey together through Advent in preparation for the great Christmas festival when we shall celebrate the coming of God among us. At some point, on Christmas Eve or Christmas Day, many of us will celebrate Holy Communion. So, we shall end with some reflections on that because, in a unique way, many of the themes are brought together at this meal.

There is something almost timeless about sharing this feast. We eat the bread and drink the wine because there is a strong historical base. Christ really did suffer and die upon the cross for our salvation. His body was broken and his blood poured out, once, for all. So we say, **'Christ has died.'**

But no part of the Christian Church believes that the Christ of God belongs only in the past. We may argue among ourselves about the form of Christ's presence in Holy Communion but none of us believes in his absence. In 'doing this in remembrance' we make his presence known. We recognise in this meal a God-given meeting-place between ourselves and God. He who died comes in communion as our contemporary to feed us spiritually. So we say, **'Christ is risen.'**

The great banquet is one of the images which the Bible uses for the completion of all things. Many will come from east and west to sit at the great feast (see Matthew 8.11). God receives his people home in joy, thankfulness and praise. This is the faith and hope we affirm as, with saints and angels and all the company of heaven, we join even now in the unending hymn of praise. So we say, **'Christ will come again.'**

As part of the service we say together the Lord's Prayer. In it we ask for our daily bread. Bread is one of the necessities of life. It represents a divine provision. One theologian has argued that no one should take the bread at Holy Communion without working for all God's children to have bread. Thus there is a connection between worship and ethics, between gift and responsibility, between our salvation and our present discipleship. Would eating the bread at Christmas Communion without a thought or act for the world's hungry amount to eating unworthily, not discerning the body (see 1 Corinthians 11.27 – 32)?

Actually, the phrase 'our daily bread' in the Lord's Prayer is a difficult one. This is the only place in the New Testament where a strange Greek word is used. Some scholars have pointed out that the request may be for 'the bread which belongs to tomorrow'. If that is so, perhaps, we have another eschatological reference as we ask God to give us today the food that belongs to the end of time. Incidentally, did you know that Bethlehem means 'house of bread'?

Coming to Holy Communion is always an important, and often a deeply enriching, experience of God.

Advent ends as we come to the table. There we find our thoughts focused in the God who came, who comes and who will come. We celebrate the truth that from the beginning of time God has been at work in history, ever making new. We celebrate the coming God in Jesus, in the babe of Bethlehem, the man of the cross and the empty tomb. And we also celebrate in anticipation God's coming from the future, to complete the **advent**ure of all his purposes and with Christians through all the ages we say, *'Maranatha'* – 'Come, Lord, come!'

A prayer

Lord, in your coming is our hope. We repent of all that frustrates your rule in us and through us. We are not worthy that you should turn to us. But in trust we rejoice, for you came in prophets' word; you come in the vulnerable baby and the man of costly love; and you will come to us tomorrow and tomorrow until the end that has no ending.

Now, as the festival draws near, we wait and in the waiting we worship; we worship and in the worship we hope; and in our hoping we trust your promise and receive your love, through Jesus Christ our Lord. Come, Lord Jesus, come! Amen.